The
Child Sexual Abuse
Custody Dispute
Annotated Bibliography

The
Child Sexual Abuse
Custody Dispute
Annotated Bibliograpy

Wendy Deaton

Suzanne Long

Holly A. Magaña

Julie Robbins

In cooperation with the
California Professional Society on the Abuse of Children

Sage Publications
International Educational and Professional Publisher
Thousand Oaks ♦ London ♦ New Delhi

For information address:

Sage Publications, Inc.
2455 Teller Road
Thousand Oaks, California 91320

Sage Publications Ltd.
6 Bonhill Street
London EC2A 4PU
United Kingdom

Sage Publications India Pvt. Ltd.
M-32 Market
Greater Kailash I
New Delhi 110 048 India

Printed in the United States of America

Library of Congress Cataloging-in-Publication Data

Deaton, Wendy.
    The child sexual abuse custody dispute annotated bibliography /
Wendy Deaton, Suzanne Long, Holly A. Magaña, Julie Robbins.
    p. cm.
    ISBN 0-8039-5861-7 (cloth)
    1. Child sexual abuse—Law and legislation—United States—Bibliography.
2. Custody of children—United States—Bibliography.
I. Title.
KF9323.A1D43 1994
016.3467301'7—dc20
[016.34730617]   94-17097
                                                                      CIP

First Printing, 1995
Managing Editor: C. A. Hoffman

INTRODUCTION

It is with great pleasure that I, along with the co-authors, am able to provide this publication for the professional community. Developing this book has taken more than two years of discussion, planning, and extensive research and writing. We owe this book to the hard work, patience, and perserverance of all those who participated.

This book came out of The Child Sexual Abuse Custody Dispute Task Force of CAPSAC (The California Professional Society on the Abuse of Children). CAPSAC is a multidisciplinary professional society dedicated to assuring a sensitive and effective response to child abuse in the state of California. One of the goals of the organization is to design and propose improved policies and systems that will better protect abused children.

At the 1990 CAPSAC retreat, the CAPSAC Board voted that child sexual abuse cases involving custody disputes were a major concern for professionals in the field. Many issues appeared to be of concern, including how cases are evaluated for court, how cases are managed, and the interaction of the juvenile, family, and criminal court system. A primary goal was to develop a protocol and policy recommendations for the management of these cases in California.

When the Task Force first developed its goals, it became clear that to tackle any one of these issues was a monumental task. Before a protocol or policy recommendations could be developed, a literature search was necessary. This search developed into the project that is now *The Child Sexual Abuse Custody Dispute Annotated Bibliography.*

This book provides summaries of literature regarding children's testimony, false allegations, research, commentary, and other supporting information in custody disputes. We hope it will be a useful resource for all professionals—legal, medical, mental health, judiciary, child protection, and law enforcement—who have any involvement with custody dispute cases.

The *Bibliography* covers literature in the legal, social, and behavioral sciences. The review is intended to cover the most significant articles in these literatures over the designated period of time. In two years, we will be providing a 2nd edition addendum that will include any missing articles and new 1992 and 1993 publications. If readers would like any further information on the Task Force or have additional publications that they want to see included in the 2nd edition, please write to

Julie Robbins, LCSW
P.O. Box #210422
San Francisco, CA 94121

Task Force members and the authors of this publication have put an enormous amount of time and energy into this project. I want to personally thank Suzanne, Wendy, and Holly for their undying dedication and the incredible work that made this project complete. I also want to thank them for putting up with my numerous phone calls asking to do "just one more article."

Thanks also to the CAPSAC Board, who supported us through this entire effort. It is with great pleasure that we donate all proceeds of this book to CAPSAC so that the organization can continue to do its excellent work in California.

A very special thanks goes to Erna Olafson, who made numerous contributions to this publication and facilitated greatly in the editing of the final draft. Without Erna, we may never have gotten the publication off the ground.

And finally, a big thanks to Jon Conte, who helped a great deal with the final editing and publication process.

I would like to dedicate this book to all children who have been sexually abused, in the hope that this takes us one step closer to their healing and one step closer to more improved intervention, treatment, and prevention by those professionals committed to helping them.

—*Julie Robbins*

CHILD SEXUAL ABUSE ALLEGATIONS
IN THE CONTEXT OF
CUSTODY/VISITATION DISPUTES

Ackerman, M. J., & Kane, A. W. (1990). *How to examine psychological experts in divorce and other civil actions* (with yearly cumulative supplements). Eau Claire, WI: Professional Educations Systems.

In the 12 pages devoted to child sexual abuse in the context of custody disputes, the authors cite 12 articles and conference presentations, primarily work that tends to disconfirm allegations of abuse. A majority of the studies reviewed are based on very small samples. As an example of the article's tendency to cite work that disconfirms abuse, Chapter Ten of the 1992 Supplement leads off with a discussion of false abuse allegations and Munchausen by Proxy Syndrome, and quotes A. Yates on erroneous allegations by preschoolers. (This appears to be the same Yates who in the 1978 *Sex Without Shame* wrote that incest can produce "erotically competent young women" and that "childhood is the best time to learn.") A concern regarding this reference is that the authors cite very few of the peer-reviewed, empirically based works such as Everson

& Boat; Thoennes & Tjaden; Sorenson & Snow; Corwin,
Sirles, Gomez-Shwartz, Finkelhor, & Williams.

Anthony, G., & Watkeys, J. (1991). False allegations
in child sexual abuse: The pattern of referral in an
area where reporting is not mandatory. *Children
and Society*, *5*(2), 111-122.

This study examines all reported cases of sexual abuse
between 1986 and 1989 in an urban area in South Wales,
where child abuse reporting is not mandatory. Four hundred ten children were referred, 350 cases were fully
investigated, and 197 cases were confirmed. Among the
unsubstantiated cases, 18% of the allegations were believed to be false, and 8.5% were apparently malicious. Of
the remaining 90 unsubstantiated cases, the authors state
that they arose out of professional or family concern rather
than as a result of a false or malicious allegation. False
allegations were less likely to occur when the initial complaint came directly from the child. The authors point out
that many of the children who made false allegations had,
in fact, been abused but had incorrectly identified the
perpetrator. The authors conclude that their study "indicates that despite the difficulties surrounding the diagnosis
of child sexual abuse, and the absence of an absolute test
in this diagnosis, the problem of direct false allegations
remains small."

Apel, S. B. (1989). Custodial parents, child sexual abuse, and the legal system: Beyond contempt. *American University Law Review, 38,* 491-529.

Vermont Law School professor Apel wrote this article while Elizabeth Morgan was still in jail for refusing to reveal the whereabouts of her daughter, Hilary, based upon Morgan's belief that the child's father, Eric Foretich, had repeatedly sexually abused the girl. The article notes the legal and cultural obstacles to proving in court that child sexual abuse has occurred. Apel contends that because of the nature of sexual abuse, the child witness is often the only source of evidence that such an assault took place, but, "The notion that children cannot be believed is entrenched in our legal system as well as the larger culture." She notes that in spite of the fact that studies show that the incidence of lying about sexual abuse by custodial mothers is apparently very low, "the myth of the vindictive female spouse remains" and that mothers who allege sexual abuse can have their fitness as parents called into question specifically because they have made such accusations. In addition, resources to investigate sexual abuse charges continue to remain very limited, and cases are often "unfounded" simply because time and resources were not available for an adequate investigation.

As a solution, Apel proposes a new standard, which she terms "the necessity defense" standard, which is meant to be applied in contempt proceedings against custodial parents such as Morgan. This standard would recognize a good faith belief that violating the court order was necessary to protect the child from further harm and that this should be a complete defense against charges of contempt. She argues that given the limitations of the legal system and the difficulty of proving allegations of child abuse, the courts would do well to honor the good faith belief of the custodial parent rather than imprisoning her, even, in her opinion, at the expense of the rights of the noncustodial parent to maintain contact with the child.

Awad, G. A. (1987). The assessment of custody and access disputes in cases of sexual abuse allegations. *Canadian Journal of Psychiatry*, *32*(7), 539-544.

The author observes that sexual abuse allegations directed at one parent can arise in the context of custody and access disputes. The role of the clinician, when such allegations occur, is to provide an assessment of the total situation, taking the allegations into account. Determining the probability that sexual abuse has occurred involves a thorough assessment of the accuser, the accused, the accusation, the child, and different family subsystems. Awad contends that particular attention should be paid to interviewing the young child, with detailed focus on the interviewing process, how the interviews are reported, and what conclusions may be drawn from them. Following a thorough assessment, the clinician may reach one of three conclusions: that the sexual abuse has probably occurred, has probably not occurred, or is unsure. A strong caution is given against becoming entangled in an endless process of trying to find out whether the allegations are true or false. Whatever conclusions are reached are but one factor in the recommendations regarding custody and/or access. Ultimately, the recommendations will be made according to the best interests of the child, taking into account the child's relationships and attachments, as well as the sexual abuse allegations. Two case vignettes are provided.

Awad, G., & McDonough, H. (1991). Therapeutic management of sexual abuse allegations in custody and visitation disputes. *American Journal of Psychotherapy, 45*(1), 113-123.

This article points out that, in many cases, trying to assess the "truthfulness" or "falseness" of sexual abuse allegations that occur in the midst of custody and access disputes may not be possible. Instead, therapeutic management of such cases is advocated. A case is presented in which sexual abuse was suspected because the recanting child displayed sexualized symptoms. Following a thorough assessment that indicated that the child was abused but could not confirm the identity of the offender, both the child and the mother were seen in psychotherapy on a regular basis. The father used counseling to achieve rights for visitations. The building of a therapeutic relationship allowed the authors to experiment with the situation until they felt they could identify the potential offender. The therapeutic relationship provided this family an alternative method of resolution rather than using the judicial system.

Ayoub, C. C., Grace, P. F., Paradise, J. E., Newberger, E. H. (1991). Alleging psychological impairment of the accuser to defend oneself against a child abuse allegation: A manifestation of wife battering and false accusation. In M. Robin (Ed.), *Assessing child maltreatment reports: The problem of false allegations* (pp. 191-207). Binghamton, NY: Haworth Press.

The authors discuss five cases involving physical and sexual abuse allegations in families where the parents had recently divorced. The allegations were made against the fathers, who denied them and alleged that the mothers' emotional stability and/or childhood history of abuse were the root of the families' problems. In all of these cases, the evaluators found that there was a history of spousal abuse and intimidation perpetrated by the fathers, which was not initially evident. The authors offer a theoretical framework for understanding the dynamics in these families and recommend that evaluators assess cases carefully for the possibility of spousal abuse and use special precautions to ensure the safety of family members.

B

Beitchman, J. H., Zucker, K. J., Hood, J. E., Granville, A.D., & Akman, D. (1991). A review of the term effects of child sexual abuse. *Child Abuse & Neglect, 15*, 537-556.

This is the first of a two-part article; the second part (1992) assesses the long-term effects. Major findings of this literature review include the following: Victims of child sexual abuse are more likely than nonvictims to develop some kind of inappropriate sexual or sexualized behavior; more severe outcomes are correlated with frequent abuse, long-term abuse, abuse with force, or penetration; and abuse by a father or stepfather. In addition, victims of sexual abuse seem to be more likely than nonvictims to come from disturbed families.

Benedek, E., & Schetky, D. H. (1985). Allegations of sexual abuse in child custody and visitation disputes. In D. H. Schetky & E. P. Benedek (Eds.), *Emerging issues in child psychiatry and the law* (pp. 145-158). New York: Brunner/Mazel.

Benedek and Schetky present data about 18 cases from their clinical and forensic practice of which they found a false allegation rate of 56% and all were allegations brought by mothers. Sample selection may figure in this high rate. Benedek and Schetky see the source of false allegations emerging primarily in the mother's personality and psychopathology, including paranoia, hysteria, borderline personality, and vindictiveness. They assert that false allegations are rare, but that they do occur, "particularly in custody cases."

Benedek, E., & Schetky, D. H. (1987). Problems in
validating allegations of sexual abuse. Part 1:
Factors affecting perception and recall of events.
*Journal of the American Academy of Child and
Adolescent Psychiatry, 26*(6), 912-915.

This article stresses the complexities involved in validating allegations of sexual abuse. It goes over developmental factors that affect ˙children's memory and
communication of past events, and reviews research on
children's recall of traumatic events and children's response to suggestions about events that did not happen. The
authors challenge the view that children never lie and point
to the developmental and emotional factors that may lead
to a child's susceptibility to parental suggestion regarding
molestation. Included is a review of interviewer techniques
and the conclusion that interviewers should be highly
trained mental health professionals, should have access to
the children on multiple occasions, and must be "objective
and open to the possibility that an accusation may be false."

Benjamin, R. (1991). Mediative strategies in the management of child sexual abuse matters. *Family &
Conciliation Courts Review, 29*, 221-245.

This article presents the supposition that when allegations of sexual abuse by a family member are made, the
child may be damaged as much by the system's response
to the abuse as by the abuse itself, if it occurred. It is
suggested that mediators can institute an approach to handle these cases that protects the child while maintaining the

integrity of the family system. Mediators are cautioned to avoid the use of words such as "victim" and "perpetrator," which suggest that fault can be determined, and to maintain an emphasis on the family system while, at the same time, paying close attention to the balance of power between the parties. It is also suggested that attorneys, therapists, and other professionals should be part of the mediation process.

Berkowitz, C. D. (1987). Sexual abuse of children and adolescents. *Advances In Pediatrics, 34,* 275-312.

Although not specific to the topic of child custody disputes, this article contains useful information regarding physical findings of sexual abuse in children and adolescents.

Berliner, L. (1988). Deciding whether a child has been sexually abused. In Nicholson & Bulkley (Eds.), *Sexual abuse allegations in custody and visitation disputes* (pp. 48-69). Washington, DC: American Bar Association.

Berliner provides a clear and detailed overview of the dilemmas facing current evaluators of child sexual abuse. She discusses the dilemmas, "How do we know if a report is accurate or if abuse really occurred? Who decides and by what criteria?" Legal fact finding and forming a professional opinion are also addressed. A review of the literature on the rates of true and false cases of sexual abuse is undertaken. Berliner concludes that fictitious reports constitute only a small fraction of reports but do happen and must be ruled out before an objective opinion can be expressed. She discusses extensively how an evaluator forms an opinion, various data necessary, tools used, and other components.

In carefully considering children's statements of abuse, a review of current information on children's memories and suggestibility is included. In interviewing children about abuse experiences, Berliner reviews non-verbal aides, anatomical dolls, procedures for interviewing, assessing for reliability and validation, considering alternative explanations for the child's statement of abuse, and custody situation complications. The author then calls for the development of special approaches for evaluating very young children, as the directed interview may not be appropriate. The very young child may require an extended period of therapeutic intervention and observation before an adequate professional opinion can be made. Berliner states that "more information from developmental experts is needed on how to best elicit information from the very young child." She urges thoughtful evaluators to "remember the limitations of their knowledge and/or resist the pressure or the temptation to be more definitive than current understanding allows."

Berliner, L. (1990). Protecting or harming? Parents who flee with their children. *Journal of Interpersonal Violence*, *5*, 119-120.

This article discusses custody or visitation disputes that involve an allegation of sexual abuse against a parent. In most instances, judicial determinations and recommendations protect children believed to have been abused by a parent. However, Berliner points out that some parents, mostly women, who have been faced with a judicial order to permit visitation or who have lost custody and believe that the other parent presents a continuing risk, have chosen to flee with their children.

Berliner, L. (1991). The questions of belief. *Journal of Interpersonal Violence, 6*, 240.

This article is a brief commentary that places in historical perspective the insistence by some professionals that children never lie about abuse. Berliner points out that, historically, there has been a collective denial of the abuse of children. Public awareness of the tremendous harm caused by violence in families has been an important accomplishment of the last several decades. She explains that "the importance of persuading a reluctant society to accept the magnitude of abuse made any challenge to the veracity of abuse reports a threat to the progress which had been made." Nonetheless, the author feels that the importance of believing a victim depends on the context. In the courtroom, it must depend on the weight of the evidence. While in the therapist's office, Berliner says, "belief is another thing."

Bischoff, K. S. (1990). The voice of a child: Independent legal representation of children in private custody disputes when sexual abuse is alleged. *University of Pennsylvania Law Review, 138,* 1383-1409.

This article makes the argument that "children must be provided with independent legal representation whenever allegations of sexual abuse are made [in family court] because neither the judge nor the child's parents can adequately represent the child's interests." The authors make the observation that children have the right to legal representation in juvenile court proceedings and point out that recent standards prepared by the American Bar Association suggest that the appointment of independent legal counsel for children should be required in all divorce related custody disputes. Two states, Wisconsin and New Hampshire, have implemented this requirement. The proper role of the child's representative is discussed. The common arguments against the appointment of an attorney for the child are reviewed and refuted.

Blick, L. C. (1989). Child custody issues in cases of suspected child sexual abuse. *The Advisor, 2*(2), 11-12.

In a simple, straightforward article, Blick outlines the factors to consider in structuring contact between a suspected child victim and the parent who has been accused of child abuse during a child custody dispute. Three crucial steps are highlighted: (a) assessing the child's willingness to see the alleged abuser, (b) evaluating the alleged abuser's readiness to see the child, and (c) structuring the context in which visits take place with the aim of supporting a safe, healthy relationship between the child and the parent. Blick strongly advocates that visits be monitored by a trained mental health professional and that the child continue in treatment with careful documentation maintained of both normal and abnormal behavior occurring before, during, and after monitored visits.

Blush, G. J., & Ross, K. L. (1987). Sexual allegations in divorce: The SAID syndrome. *Conciliation Courts Review, 25*(1), 1-11.

The authors suggest that clinicians and others working in child advocacy positions may fail to recognize what they consider to be the important dynamics of sexual abuse allegations in divorce (SAID) syndrome that occur at the time of pre- or postdivorce conflict. The authors recommend the following in the evaluation of sexual abuse allegations in custody dispute cases: (a) The professional should take the position of clinical investigator, rather than clinical therapist, during the initial stages of contact with potential SAID families and children. This will assist in avoiding the pitfall of a therapeutic alliance with children or a complaining parent that could potentially result in a distorted perspective. (b) The professional should pay particular attention to the time sequence and context surrounding the initial allegation and to the personality profiles of the complaining parent, the child, and the alleged perpetrator. Although some of the conclusions drawn by the authors regarding the credibility and validity issues may be controversial, the emphasis on the use of a sound investigative procedure and on consideration of the special circumstances surrounding divorce are useful.

Blush, G. J., & Ross, K. L. (1990). Investigation and case management issues and strategies. *Issues in Child Abuse Accusations*, 2(3), 152-160.

From their experience, the authors discuss child sexual abuse allegations in the context of custody and visitation disputes. They express concern that these cases are often mismanaged and misunderstood, causing harm to the parties involved. Loss of control by the management agency or the individual professional in the beginning stages of the allegation characterize many cases that, according to the authors, turn out to be false. Mistakes in these types of cases are highlighted. Case management problems are detailed, and more effective management suggestions are made. The use of a multidisciplinary team is recommended, and the uses of specific interviewing goals and objectives are discussed. One recommendation is that the interviewer offer the alleged perpetrator the opportunity to tell his or her story and to be able to answer to the allegations of the accusing adult or child directly. The authors explore the use of this confrontive modality as a case management procedure, as well as other recommendations.

Bresee, P., Stearns, G., Bess, B., & Packer, L. (1986). Allegations of child sexual abuse in child custody disputes: A therapeutic model. *American Journal of Orthopsychiatry*, *56*, 560-569.

This article sets forth guidelines for judges and others who must make decisions in custody disputes that include allegations of child sexual abuse. The focus is on the protection of the child, and the model highlights the role of mental health professionals, prescribing separate therapists for child and parent where possible. Allegations of sexual abuse are seen as an indicator of emotional risk for the child, even in cases where the allegations are untrue.

Brooks, C. M., & Milchman, M. S. (1991). Child sexual abuse allegations during custody litigation: Conflicts between mental health expert witnesses and the law. *Behavioral Sciences and the Law*, *9*, 21-33.

This article describes a case study of sexual abuse allegations in a family where there had been a recent divorce. The mother of a 3-year-old boy alleged that the child had been sexually abused by his father during court ordered visitation. Several mental health professionals consulted on the case and offered differing opinions, one finding that the child had been sexually abused while the other concluded that the other therapist had influenced the mother to believe the child had been molested. The Court found that the child had not been molested and reinstated the father's visitation. Several years later, the father was indicted on criminal charges of sexual abuse. The article discusses the critical issues involved in the evaluation of sexual abuse allegations and suggests that the mental health professional must use a clinical research paradigm rather than a clinical diagnostic paradigm. As a result of the case described in this article, a multidisciplinary research project was initiated in the state of New Jersey with the goal of developing an objective behavioral assessment instrument for evaluating sexual abuse allegations. The article discusses briefly the initial efforts toward the development of the instrument.

Bross, D. (1992). Assumptions about child sexual abuse allegations at or about the time of divorce: A commentary. *Journal of Child Sexual Abuse*, *1*(2), 115-116.

Guardian ad litem and author Bross responds and comments on the issue, as has Judge Schudson and Attorney Toth. Recognizing that each case needs very careful and thorough assessment, he refers to research by Jones & McGraw (1987) and their "honest appraisal of the difficulty of knowing enough in many instances to feel very secure with the decisions which must be made." Jones & McGraw went on to develop a paradigm for looking at allegations in custody or visitation. They propose that "The following levels of confidence be used: definitely true, probably true, possibly true, possibly false, probably false, and definitely false. Only cases that were definitely or probably true would be treated clinically as 'cases.' " Bross commends their restraint in approaching the issue and recommends that professionals model similar behavior of reserving judgment.

Bross describes a useful way of handling those cases in which no one can determine whether the child has or has not been abused. He notes the importance of providing sanctuary for the child caught in the mire created by one or both parents. Having a therapist for the child has been useful. He also points out that " the therapist is not required to talk to any attorney, judge or parent unless the best interests of the child require it." This approach has tended to quiet the controversy and provide protection. Evidence of abuse may then be brought out through the process of the continuing therapeutic relationship, and manipulation, if present, by either parent may then surface.

Bulkley, J. (1988). The child's input in custody and visitation disputes involving sexual abuse allegations. In Nicholson & Bulkley (Eds.), *Sexual abuse allegations in custody and visitation cases* (pp. 214-229). Washington, DC: American Bar Association.

This chapter studies the child's input in custody and visitation disputes involving sexual abuse allegations. Children in custody disputes are often asked to provide testimony in which the judge interviews the child privately in chambers. Most jurisdictions require special due process protections for judicial interviewing of children in custody hearings. Procedural safeguards should be instituted in obtaining information from the child in custody and visitation disputes involving sexual abuse allegations. Although the child's preference is considered, it usually is not given controling weight. The author emphasizes that there are few of these protections because "arguably the loss of custody may not be significant enough to invoke due process as long as visitation rights are retained." However, the loss of both custody and visitation, which may result from an allegation of sexual abuse in a custody hearing, "is not much different than termination of parental rights that may occur in a juvenile court action, where procedural protections usually exist."

C

Conte, J. R., Sorenson, E., Fogarty, L., & Rosa, J. D. (1991). Evaluating children's reports of sexual abuse: Results from a survey of professionals. *American Journal of Orthopsychiatry, 61,* 428-437.

A group of 212 professionals with a mean length of experience interviewing children about sexual abuse of 8.8 years were studied regarding their procedure for validating children's sexual abuse allegations. This group included 84 child protection services workers, 98 mental health professionals, and 30 other professionals (law enforcement officers, state attorneys, and so on). Of the sample, 79%

were female and 21% were male; 56% had master's degrees and 18%, Ph.Ds. The study explored which behavioral, physical, and emotional indicators of abuse influenced the decisions of professionals and identified their beliefs about why children might make false allegations of sexual abuse.

The results were that about half of the sample interview the child first, half interview the nonoffending parent first, and 82% sometimes or often interview the alleged offender directly. Of the latter, 34% use psychological tests. Ninety percent of the respondents agreed that being the subject of a custody battle could distort a child's report, and 13% reported that, in their experience, this often happens. The overwhelming majority (96%) usually do not interview the child in the presence of the alleged offender. The most important criteria for validation were listed as physical indicators, age-inappropriate sexual knowledge, sexualized play, and child interview characteristics, such as consistency over time, idiosyncratic detail, and disclosures about pressure or coercion.

The conclusion of the study is that although there is professional agreement regarding which validation criteria may be important in determining the credibility of sexual abuse disclosures involving children, the dependability of such criteria still requires additional research and discussion.

Cooke, G., & Cooke, M. (1991). Dealing with sexual abuse allegations in the context of custody evaluations. *American Journal of Forensic Psychology, 9*(3), 55-67.

The authors describe assessment techniques for evaluating sexual abuse allegations that arise in the context of custody evaluations. They point out that false allegations may be more likely to occur in this context and suggest strategies for assessing this possibility. The first recommendation is that evaluators must always be independent and objective and should be appointed by the court or by agreement of both parents. A minimum of three to five sessions with the child is recommended. They recommend that both parents be interviewed about the allegation, the circumstances under which the molestation was first mentioned be explored, the various possible sources of incorrect reports be considered, and an assessment for the Parent Alienation Syndrome described by Gardner be made. Psychological testing results are of minimal utility, and the evaluation should express cautions about their limitations. Once a determination has been made regarding the likelihood that abuse occurred, the implications for custodial arrangements must be considered. The authors suggest that "if it is determined that there is a high probability that the allegation was deliberately fabricated, serious consideration must be given to [that] parent's motives and possible negative impact on the child."

Corwin, D. L. (1988). Early diagnosis of child sexual abuse: Diminishing the lasting effects. In G. E. Wyatt & G. J. Powell (Eds.), *Lasting effects of child sexual abuse*. Newbury Park, CA: Sage.

This paper summarizes the results of a "Summit Conference" called in 1985 to put together diagnostic criteria for a "Sexually Abused Child's Disorder" for inclusion by the DSM III-R committee but not included in the DSM III-R. It offers a model that is still useful and has been corroborated in many respects by subsequent comparative research.

Corwin, D. L., Berliner, L., Goodman, G., Goodwin, J., & White, S. (1987). Child custody disputes: No easy answers. *Journal of Interpersonal Violence, 2*, 91-105.

This article criticizes earlier work by Green and others about the assessment of false allegations during custody disputes and cautions against constructing premature evaluation criteria based on small, biased, and possibly miscategorized clinical samples. The authors distinguish between unsubstantiated or unfounded allegations (those for which insufficient evidence is available) and false or fictitious allegations (those based on misinterpretations or deliberate fabrications). They address the fact that Green's sample from which he derived his 36% false allegation statistic was made up of 11 cases from his own practice. The 4 cases Green found to be false were based entirely on his clinical impressions; there was no independent corroboration. The authors analyze one of the 4 cases classified by Green as false and offer additional evidence suggesting that the allegations may have been true and the case miscategorized. They cite studies that indicate that the sexual abuse of young children may be more frequent in the context of marital dissolution than otherwise and suggest that marital separation may also permit disclosure of existing abuse. The authors warn of potential hazards associated with the standard practice of interviewing the alleged child victim in the presence of the alleged perpetrator. The authors also express concern regarding their perception of possible gender bias.

Corwin, D. L., & Olafson, E. (1993). *Child Abuse & Neglect, 17*, 1-185.

As a special issue on the assessment of child sexual abuse, this collection of articles addresses a variety of subjects about child abuse assessment, including the assessment of molesters, psychological testing, developmental issues, dissociative disorders, child drawings, information processing of trauma, and other subjects of relevance to the assessment of child sexual abuse in custody dispute cases.

Cramer, J. (March, 1991). Why children lie in court. *Time.*

This article prompted replies by researcher Gail S. Goodman and John E. Showalter, president of the American Academy of Child and Adolescent Psychiatry, which were published in the letters section on April 1, 1991, as well as a critique from the APSAC board, not printed in *Time* but printed on the front page of the Spring, 1991, *APSAC Advisor.*

Cramer's article relied heavily on the work of Green (1986), to the exclusion of other experts in the field. Cramer reported that Green's study was "conducted by the American Academy of Child Psychiatry." As Dr. Schowalter, President of the Academy, pointed out in his letter, the Academy does not conduct clinical studies. In addition, Schowalter wrote, by applying Green's 4 out of 11 children's false allegation statistic of 36% as a generalization, "Cramer makes an error with potentially terrible implications for children who are abused." Goodman also wrote to correct that Cramer had left out her research with Saywitz. She pointed out that Cramer "failed to highlight the fact that the children's most common error, by far, was underreporting of genital touch" and that, in general, the children she and Saywitz studied were highly resistant to suggestions of abuse. Goodman also stated that none of the studies Cramer cited prove that children often make unfounded sexual abuse charges.

D

Damon, L., Card, J., & Todd, J. (1992). Incest in young children. In Ammerman & Hersen (Eds.), *Assessment of family violence: A clinical and legal sourcebook* (pp. 148-172). New York: Wiley.

The authors of this chapter focus thoroughly on how to conduct family and child interviews when assessing for incest in young children 4 to 12 years of age. The following issues are addressed: disclosure of the secret, fears and threats, guilt and shame, coercion, retraction, and the developmental limitations of the young child. Various assessment protocols and procedures are covered. The authors highlight the importance of legal considerations when conducting these assessments, including the research on false allegations, leading questions and suggestibility, memory, and anatomical dolls.

Repeatedly emphasized is the need for evaluators to have special skills and knowledge of child development, to be able to use age-appropriate language, and to be able to build rapport with children. Evaluators must have current knowledge of the literature regarding theory and research on memory, suggestibility, medical findings, and dynamics of sexual abuse. Also stressed is the need to update knowledge of the legal ramifications of the interview format, along with consulting with professionals to coordinate and facilitate the process of child protection. The authors remind evaluators that it is of the utmost importance that they proceed cautiously, weighing all information carefully before forming an opinion. Evaluators must eliminate all other possible alternative explanations when there are allegations of incest and, above all, interviewers must remain unbiased.

Deed, M. (1991). Court-ordered child custody evaluations: Helping or victimizing vulnerable families. *Psychotherapy*, *28*(1), 76-84.

This article addressed the psychologist in the role of court-ordered evaluator in cases of child custody disputes. Some significant points made by the author refer to the critical need for psychologists in this role to be fully informed regarding a variety of subjects, including certain legal concepts, relevant law as it applies in a variety of cases, the realities of custody litigation and the effect that long-term litigation processes may have on deteriorating functioning within the family, the limitations of the court system, the social and economic realities of divorce, the dynamics of child sexual abuse, and the content and extent of their own personal and professional biases.

Some of the areas discussed include a discussion that definitions of sexual abuse of children may differ in different legal and judicial contexts, and knowledge of relevant law pertaining to abuse is critical for the protection of the children involved in custody cases. The author also points out that for the psychologist, truth is equivalent to reality. In the context of the law, "truth" can only be produced through trial. "Truth" does not necessarily coincide with reality; right and morality are irrelevant. "Truth" is a legal construct that relates to facts as they emerge at trial.

The authors particularly caution the psychologist in the role of court-ordered evaluator to remain fully cognizant of their own personal and professional biases and of the potential pitfalls of forming the dual relationship of evaluator and therapist to the same family. Therapist is the role of "working out" the custody, while the evaluator, most usefully, serves to offer objective recommendations or options to the court. In this regard, the issue of joint custody decisions should be reviewed, and note should be taken that the most recent research indicates that when joint custody is imposed while parents remain psychologically embattled, these children have the poorest post-divorce outcome.

The author advocates that the American Psychological Association establish a task force on custody evaluation to assist in examining the relevant issues and to issue guidelines for psychologists who are interested in engaging in this controversial and challenging field.

DeYoung, M. (1986). A conceptual model for judging the truthfulness of a young child's allegation of sexual abuse. *American Journal of Orthopsychiatry, 56*, 550-559.

After briefly outlining the long history of skepticism about child sexual abuse allegations, DeYoung discusses the alleged "children never lie" phase and the reaction against it within the McMartin and Jordan preschool cases. She then observes that the current backlash "is reminiscent of the historical skepticism, and seems to challenge the very wisdom of categorizing the abuse as a social problem at all." Because the greatest doubt seems to be about accusations by very young children, DeYoung presents a sequence of investigative steps for judging the truthfulness of children between 2 and 7, taking into account developmental issues.

DeYoung's developmental focus serves to refine conceptual models that do not adjust for age, such as those by Faller (1988) and Raskin & Esplin (1991). She notes that clarity, for example, is affected by preoperational cognitive characteristics that would cause a child to describe ejaculation as urination (objects defined by function) or to believe that an erect penis is not a penis at all (lack of conservations characteristics in the preoperational stage). She also notes that because of the developmental features of a young child's perception of time, this is one elaborated detail that is likely to be confused and inconsistent, especially since psychic trauma can interfere with time perception.

As for indicators of sexual abuse, DeYoung cautions against the premature formulation of symptoms lists and recommends the application of the Finkelhor & Browne model. With reference to lying, she states that being pressured by an adult to fabricate a sexual abuse allegation will produce symptoms of stress, but that these symptoms are likely to be different from those formulated by Finkelhor & Browne.

Staff. (1988). Deliberate false allegations of child sexual abuse possible in 14% of custody cases. *Directions*, 2(26).

This nine paragraph 1988 article attempts to briefly summarize Thoennes's research as she revealed some findings to an American Orthopsychiatric Association Annual Meeting. Only 2% of over 9,000 custody and visitation

disputes studied involved any type of sexual abuse allegation. In 14% of 58 cases there was concern raised about the
possibility that the allegation might be a deliberate false
report with intention to manipulate custody/visitation
agreements. Other articles on this same research cover the
material more completely and with greater depth.

Doris, J. (1991). *The suggestibility of children's*
recollections: Implications for eyewitness testi-
mony. Washington, DC: American Psychological Association.

This book was based in part on a 1989 Cornell University
Conference looking at the suggestibility of children's recollections, a subject known to be controversial because of issues
related to the believability of children as witnesses. John Doris
edited this book of 10 chapters, representing an exchange of
information and debate between leading psychologists who
have differences of opinion on the subject of children's suggestibility. The researchers differ in methods they use, as well
as in the interpretation of the results. Topics include the
development of memory, the effects of stress on the child
witness, and suggestibility of children's testimony with implications for sexual abuse investigations. Current controversial issues are debated and future research topics are
considered.

Eastman, A. M., & Moran, T. J. (1991). Multiple perspectives: Factors related to differential diagnosis of sex abuse and divorce trauma in children under six. In M. Robin (Ed.), *Assessing child maltreatment reports: The problem of false allegations* (pp. 159-175). Binghamton, NY: Haworth Press.

This chapter reviews research that evaluates the developmental consequences of divorce and sexual abuse for children under 6 years old. It offers a systematic basis from which to evaluate children's adjustment reaction within a unified developmental perspective. A clinical guide to comprehensive assessment questions is provided. These questions focus on historical and divorce adjustment factors as they relate to parent-child relationships, the crisis of abuse and disclosure, and crisis resolution. The assessment complexities of a nationally publicized case are described to illustrate the difficulty of differential diagnosis and the importance of examining multiple variables. In addition, another case example is presented to illustrate the use of a team of professionals to help divorced parents work cooperatively to establish a safe visitation plan.

Edwards, L. P. (1987). The relationship of family and juvenile courts in child abuse cases. *Santa Clara Law Review*, *27*, 201-279.

Judge Edwards points out that family court was not designed to protect children from parental abuse and neglect and that custody/visitation cases should be referred to juvenile courts early in the process when they involve serious abuse allegations. He also recommends that courts adhere to established guidelines to manage child abuse cases more effectively and to stay within their original mandates.

Edwards, L. P. (1989). *Family and juvenile court management of child abuse cases.* Paper presented to the Marin (California) Family Law Bar Association.

This paper outlines procedures to follow if child abuse allegations come to the attention of Family Court Services staff during a family law proceeding. This includes child protection reporting and steps to be followed if the child protection agency does not respond within 10 days. It also recommends suspension of custody and visitation proceedings and states that the Family Court shall resume custody and visitation litigation only after written authorization by the Juvenile Court.

Ekman, M.A.M. (1989). Kids' testimony in court: The sexual abuse crisis. In P. Ekman (Ed.), *Why kids lie: How parents can encourage truthfulness* (pp. 152-180). New York: Penguin.

Ekman cites impressions by judges in Alameda and San Diego Counties that sex abuse charges occur in as many as 10% of custody cases that come to court. She states that "researchers have now learned" that children do sometimes lie about sexual abuse and that this is "more likely to occur in custody disputes, where they are influenced by one parent against another." She cites a *New York Times* story about the University of Michigan Family and Law program stating that more than half of sexual abuse allegations in custody cases are untrue. Ekman quotes a *New York Times* article that apparently attributes the 1988 article by Jones and Seig to Krugman.

A lawyer who is critical of joint custody orders, Ekman believes that courts should return to maternal preference for custody of young children. She also cites G. Melton and others who warn about the limits of mental health expertise in forensic sexual abuse work. Ekman is currently at work on a history of custody law and practice in the United States.

Ekman, P. (1989). *Why kids lie: How parents can encourage truthfulness.* New York: Penguin.

A popular book for parents by the leading American expert on nonverbal indicators of lying (*Telling Lies*, new edition, 1992). It is useful in outlining the research about developmental issues with respect to children's lies. A family production, this book contains chapters by Ekman's son and by his wife, lawyer Mary Ann Mason Ekman (see previous listing). Ekman is at the University of California in San Francisco, and Mason is at the University of California in Berkeley.

Ekman, P. (1989, July/August). Would a child lie? *Psychology Today*, pp. 62-65.

In this brief adaptation of sections from *Why Kids Lie*, Ekman argues that children can deliberately lie as early as age 4 or even younger and that they know that such behavior is "bad." He cites research showing that at age 5, 92% of children state that it is always wrong to lie, whereas by age 11, only 28 % believe this. Eleven-year-olds believe that whether a lie is wrong depends on the situation. Ekman notes that research has not yet determined whether children increase or decrease their lying with age. He states that some research shows that both peer pressure and lying may peak at early adolescence and then subside. Ekman notes that his research has shown that although there are some behavioral clues to lying, most adults are fooled most of the time by lies.

Everson, M. D., & Boat, B. W. (1989). False allegations of sexual abuse by children and adolescents. *Journal of the American Academy of Child and Adolescent Psychiatry*, *28*, 230-235.

This study explored the relationship between substantiation rates and attitudes about the trustworthiness of child reports by CPS workers in North Carolina. The study found a false allegations rate of between 4.7% and 7.6%, which is consistent with rates found in other studies. However, the study showed that a subset of CPS workers who are predisposed against believing child and adolescent claims of sexual abuse arrive at significantly lower substantiation rates in their caseloads than those not skeptically predisposed. This article, like all the work by Everson and Boat, is rigorously done and carefully argued.

Everson, M. D., & Boat, B. W. (1990). Sexualized doll play among young children: Implications for the use of anatomical dolls in sexual abuse evaluations. *Journal of the American Academy of Child and Adolescent Psychiatry, 29,* 736-742.

This study examined the extent of sexualized play with sexually anatomically correct dolls by over 200 non-abused children. The investigators found a 6% incidence of demonstrations of apparent sexual intercourse. They interpret their results as evidence that "anatomical dolls are not overly suggestive to young, sexually naive children, but are useful in assessing sexual knowledge and exposure to sexual intercourse."

Everson, M. D., Boat, B. W., & Robertson, K. R. (1992, January). Beliefs about the frequency of false allegations of child sexual abuse: Where you stand depends upon where you sit. Paper pre-

sented at the San Diego Conference on Responding to Child Maltreatment, San Diego, California.

This paper was designed to explore the perceptions of
professionals involved in investigation and adjudication of
child sexual abuse. Fifty-eight district court judges, 68 law
enforcement officers, 67 child protection services workers,
and 51 mental health professionals were surveyed regarding their perceptions of the frequency of false allegations
of sexual abuse by children and adolescents. District court
judges and law enforcement officers were found to be
significantly more skeptical of children's reports than were
CPS workers or mental health professionals. Those with
higher numbers of child sexual abuse cases within the prior
year were more likely to believe children than professionals with fewer cases. Across all four professional groups,
males and younger children were seen as more credible
than females or adolescents. Adolescent females were seen
as the least credible by a significant margin.

Faller, K. C. (1988). Criteria for judging the credibility
of children's statements about their sexual abuse.
Child Welfare, 67, 389-401.

In this important study, Faller tested standard criteria
for evaluating interviews (context, description of the
abuse, and emotional reactions) on 103 cases confirmed by

the perpetrator confession or partial confession. She found that 68% contained all three criteria, 10.7% contained only one criterion, and almost 6% of these confirmed cases contained none of the three characteristics. This result serves as a warning that null interview findings do not disconfirm abuse. Faller also found that boys were less likely than girls to meet two of the three criteria and that younger children were less able than older children to describe the abuse in detail.

Faller, K. C. (1988). The myth of the "collusive mother": Variability in the functioning of mothers of victims of intrafamilial sexual abuse. *Journal of Interpersonal Violence, 3,* 190-196.

This study compared 171 mothers whose children were sexually victimized by three different types of father figures on factors related to maternal collusion. Data were gathered in 1978-1986 from cases seen at a university treatment center. Categories were mothers whose children were abused by biological fathers married to the mothers, by stepfathers and mothers' live-in partners, and by non-custodial fathers where there was a separation or divorce. Variables related to collusion that were explored are maternal protectiveness when made aware of the sexual abuse, mothers' relationship with the victim, and maternal dependency. Mothers who were separated or divorced from the offender were rated the most positively on all 3 variables. Mothers in the other 2 groups were rated about equally, but findings do not support a conclusion that they are collusive in the sexual abuse of their children. Eleven references, 3 tables, author's abstract.

Faller, K. C. (1990). Sexual abuse by paternal caretakers. In A. L. Horton, B. L. Johnson, L. M. Roundy, & D. Williams (Eds.), *The incest perpetrator: A family member no one wants to treat.* Newbury Park, CA: Sage.

This article presents data on sexual abuse seemingly triggered by the stresses of divorce. In three fourths of Faller's sample of 69 confirmed cases of sexual abuse during visitation, the mother had initiated the marital breakup. Victims were significantly younger, and boys were more likely to be abused than in other forms of paternal incest. Faller suggests that retaliatory rage against the mother, the seeking of affection and comfort from the child, and the loss of household structure, rules, and routines contribute to the pattern of paternal sexual abuse initiated during visitation.

Faller, K. C. (1990). *Understanding child sexual maltreatment.* Newbury Park, CA: Sage.

Kathleen Faller states that the purpose of the book is "to serve as a resource for mental health professionals who must address the problem of child sexual abuse." The book serves as a basic reference work with a good summary of recent abuse/custody issues and research. It is the 28-page chapter "Sexual Abuse Allegations in Divorce" that has the most relevance to this bibliography. Faller addresses the dynamics leading to an allegation in divorce cases, strategies for evaluating allegations, strategies for protecting the child, research on false allegations, and conclusions. Other chapters include: Mental Health Professionals and Child Sexual Maltreatment, Defining and Understanding Child Sexual Maltreatment, Working with Protective Services and the Police, Collaborating with Attorneys, Deciding Whether or Not Sexual Abuse Has Occurred, Risk Assessment in Child Sexual Maltreatment, Sexual Abuse in Foster Family Care, Sexual Abuse in Day Care, and Sexual Abuse Allegations in Divorce.

Faller, K. C. (1991). Possible explanations for child sexual abuse allegations in divorce. *American Journal Of Orthopsychiatry, 6*, 86-91.

A summary of Faller's current work that might, because of its brevity and clarity, be read by judges. One of three studies with a respectable sample size (136) that addresses the issue of deliberate fabrication. Four classes of child sexual abuse cases in divorce are proposed: divorce precipitated by discovery of sexual abuse, long-standing sexual victimization revealed after marital breakup, sexual abuse precipitated by marital dissolution, and false allegations made during or after divorce. Implications for clinical practice are discussed. In Faller's sample of 136, she found three possible fabrications, for a rate of 2%.

Faller, K. C. (1992). Can therapy induce false allegations of sexual abuse? *APSAC Advisor*, 5(3), pp.
3-6.

Kathleen Faller is a professor at the University of
Michigan. She is a researcher and a clinician, specializing
in the area of child sexual abuse for the past 15 years. The
author examines the impact of therapy on children's
memories of sexual abuse. She points out that the concern
that therapy may cause children to think they have been
abused when they have not been should be understood in
the context of adult needs to deny that children are sexually
abused and of adult identification with the alleged abusers.
Research on children's memories is reviewed, and the
author concludes that it is rare for children to erroneously
state that they have been abused. When children are told
not to tell about an event, a considerable number remain
silent. Some children need specific questions to trigger
their memories, and children generally give accurate information in response to yes-no questions. On the other hand,
some research has found that children's memories may be
contaminated by misleading information and that "children's interpretation of ambiguous events can be manipulated and altered by an authority figure who insists upon a
particular explanation." The author concludes that the risk
of therapy causing or contaminating children's memories
is low, but therapists should be aware of the findings on
children's suggestibility and the particular contexts in
which false reports are more likely to occur.

Faller, K. C., Fronig, M., & Lipsvsky, J. (1991). The parent-child interview: Use in evaluating child allegations of sexual abuse by the parent. *American Journal of Orthopsychiatry*, *61*, 552-557.

Kathleen Faller states that "the practice of using parent-child interviews to determine whether children have been sexually abused by the parent is called into question. The relevant literature is reviewed and practical and ethical reasons for eschewing such interviews are discussed. Three case examples in which parent-child interviews were attempted or employed are described and discussed. The three cases illustrate that parent-child interviews are potentially traumatic and can be misleading. The authors feel strongly that the use of conjoint interviews in sexual abuse cases should be reconsidered by those who use them routinely . . . No studies to date have demonstrated how parent-child interactions in sexually abusive and nonabusive relationships can be reliably differentiated."

Farr, V. L., & Yuille, J. C. (1988). Assessing credibility. *Preventing Sexual Abuse*, *1*(11), 8-12.

This article briefly traces the history of attitudes toward child sexual abuse, from Freudian denial to the swing in attitude arising from the women's liberation movement and victim advocacy groups that "children do not lie about sexual abuse." The authors state that research indicates a recent feature of children's disclosures has been an increase in the rate of false allegations of abuse. They cite

Goodwin, Sahd, & Rada (1978) and Peters (1978) for earlier rates. The largest sample cited, the Jones & McGraw 1987 study, was based on 1,983 cases and had a fictitious rate of 6%. The authors' assertion that false allegation rates are increasing is based on the small, nonrandom, private clinical samples by Benedek & Schetky (1985), Green (1986), and Schuman (1987). The authors also state, without providing supporting data, that false allegation rates are more frequent in the context of custody/visitation disputes.

The authors note that because of the "increasing number" of sexual abuse allegations in the context of divorce, the response of some professionals has been to develop a bias that, in such cases, the child is probably lying. They list five reasons why children may lie: encouragement from a bitter or vindictive adult, as a response to suggestive questioning; the influence of a delusional adult, motivated by the child's own anger or resentment; and pathology in the child. They also point out, however, (as Corwin, Faller, and others have done) that divorce-related stress may trigger sexually abusive behavior or parental separation may free a child to disclose ongoing abuse.

Because there are occasions when children do lie about sexual abuse, the authors recommend the use of the Statement Reality Analysis Procedure, "which has been reliably employed for over thirty years in court-mandated assessments of the truthfulness of children's testimony in East and West Germany and Sweden." They note that the modified procedure, being researched in the United States and Canada, is called Statement Validity Analysis, and they then present the procedure (see the review of Yuille, 1988, for a brief description of SVA).

Finkelhor, D. (1986). *A sourcebook on child sexual abuse*. Beverly Hills, CA: Sage.

In this volume, a leading child sexual abuse researcher and his colleagues review research on several aspects of child sexual abuse. The first chapter reviews studies of prevalence rates. The authors explore various explanations for the wide range in reported rates (from 6% to 62% for females and from 3% to 31% for males). They found that the way subjects were asked about sexual abuse was the factor most consistently related to the rate of abuse found. The second chapter reviews research on factors that may place children at high risk for sexual abuse. The authors conclude that females are more likely to be victimized, with 2.5 females victimized for every male. Among all of the other factors studied, variables measuring the quality of the child's relationship with parents are the best predictors of sexual abuse.

The next two chapters review the research on perpetrators. A model is presented that proposes that all of the following four factors must be present in order for an adult to molest a child: (a) There must be a fit between emotional needs of the adult and the characteristics of children; (b) the adult must be sexually aroused by children; (c) the adult must be blocked from satisfying emotional and sexual needs in adult relationships; and (d) the adult must be disinhibited from breaking the social prohibitions against molestation.

The initial and long-term effects of sexual abuse are discussed in chapters five and six. The discussion is confined to the effects on females. Relevant research is reviewed in Chapter five, while Chapter six presents a conceptual framework for understanding the effects in terms of four traumatogenic dynamics: traumatic sexualization, betrayal, powerlessness, and stigmatization. The final chapters offer recommendations for designing future research and a review of research on prevention and prevention programs.

Friedrich, W. N., Grambasch, P., Broughton, D., Kuiper, J., & Beilke, R. L. (1991). Normative sexual behavior in children. *Pediatrics, 88,* 456-453.

This is a large-scale, community-based study of 880 2- through 12-year-old children screened to exclude those with a history of sexual abuse. Mothers rated child behaviors using several questionnaires, including Friedrich's Child Sexual Behavior Inventory. The results were correlated with family variables such as socioeconomic variable, age, gender, and family habits of nudity. Aggressive sexual behaviors and behaviors imitative of adults were found to be rare. Younger children were found to be more sexual than older children. Establishing norms about sexual behavior by nonabused children is clearly essential in order to determine which child sexual behaviors are abnormal and which are developmentally normal.

Gardner, R. A. (1987). *The parental alienation syndrome and the differentiation between fabricated*

and genuine child sexual abuse. Cresskill, NJ: Creative Therapeutics.

Gardner, R. A. (1989). Differentiating between bona fide and fabricated allegations of sexual abuse of children. *Journal of the American Academy of Matrimonial Lawyers*, 5, 1-26.

Gardner, R. A. (1991). *Sex abuse hysteria: Salem witch trials revisited.* Cresskill, NJ: Creative Therapeutics.

Gardner, R. A. (1992, June 19) Child sex abuse cases can be witch hunts. Letter, *New York Times*, p. A14.

The works of Columbia psychiatrist Richard Gardner are often cited in court cases. It is important to point out, however, that his work is privately printed and generally not peer-reviewed. Moreover, Gardner does not include in his references most of the growing literature about sexual abuse allegations in custody disputes from peer-reviewed professional journals.

Gardner asserts, without providing supporting data, that the vast majority of children in custody disputes fabricate when they make allegations of sexual abuse. This conclusion is contrary to the conclusions reached in studies with large samples and professionally accepted research procedures, such as the work of Thoennes & Tjaden, Hlady, Faller, and others.

In his 1987 book, he offers an "instrument," the "Sex Abuse Legitimacy Scale," which has no reliability or validity data and does not meet the minimal professional standards for a mental health instrument. The "scale" measures parental as well as child characteristics, and the mere presence of a custody dispute is counted as "very differentiating" in favor of the fabrication hypothesis. Gardner does not include Faller's (and others') work showing why allegations of actual abuse may increase at the time of divorce.

In his *Parental Alienation Syndrome* book, Gardner describes "a disturbance in which children are preoccupied with depreciation and criticism of a parent, denigration that is unjustified and/or exaggerated. The concept includes conscious, sub-conscious and unconscious factors within the programming parent that contribute to the child's alienation from the other." He sees manifestations of this in 90% of the children involved in custody conflicts.

In his 1991 book, he minimizes the seriousness and impact of child sexual assault, observing that "non-coercive pedophilia" is common in many societies, that the sexual fondling of children is "probably an ancient tradition," and that "there is a bit of pedophilia in every one of us." In his 1992 letter, he cites his own publications and claims that we are witnessing a "wave of hysteria" in sex abuse accusations that has resulted in unconstitutionally cruel and unusual punishments to those accused.

Gomes-Schwartz, B., Horowitz, J. M., & Cardarelli, A. P. (1990). *Child sexual abuse: The initial effects*. Newbury Park, CA: Sage.

This recent publication presents results of a study of 156 sexually abused children referred to the Tufts New

England Family Crisis Program. Most victims were pre-pubertal at the time of referral; 78% were female. Among other results, this study challenges the myth of the "collusive mother" in incest families. Only a minority of mothers fit the nonprotective, punitive stereotype described in much of the earlier literature. (See also Faller [*Journal of Interpersonal Violence*, 1988] on "collusive" mothers.

Goodman, G., Aman, C., & Hirschman, J. (1987). Child sexual and physical abuse: Children's testimony. In S. J. Ceci, M. P. Toglia, & D. F. Ross (Eds.), *Children's eyewitness memory* (pp. 1-23). New York: Springer-Verlag.

The authors compare findings from older "eyewitness testimony" research to more recent research involving children as active participants. In recent efforts, conditions that mimic child abuse situations are used to assess the ability of young children to accurately recall personally meaningful events. Relevance of demographic factors and degree of involvement are discussed.

Findings of the review include: (a) children's memories for central or core information is more accurate than for peripheral details, (b) memory for actions is superior to memory for the room or persons involved, (c) stress does not appear to significantly interfere with recall, (d) 3-year-olds are at a distinct disadvantage in memory recall and resistance to suggestibility compared to older children, and (e) although the children in these studies demonstrated greater susceptibility to suggestions than adults, no child in the studies made a false allegation of child abuse even when asked questions that might be inclined to foster such a report.

Goodman, G., & Clarke-Stewart, A. (1991). Suggestibility in children's testimony: Implications for sexual abuse investigations. In J. Doris (Ed.), *The suggestibility of children's recollections: Implications for eyewitness testimony* (pp. 92-105). Washington, DC: American Psychological Association.

The authors explain that the numerous studies described in this chapter "represent two independent efforts by researchers and associates to explore more directly issues of children's suggestibility in relation to sexual abuse cases." The studies are "not so much concerned with simulating abusive events as they are with testing the claim that nonabused children can be led by adult interviewers to make false reports of abuse when nothing sexual or traumatic happened." The authors state that "despite strong claims by both sides, ecologically valid and scientifically sound research to determine whether, when, and to what extent children's testimony in such cases is accurate or is influenced by suggestive questioning has been virtually nonexistent." A review of recent reseach is included with findings and conclusions. This is a most significant summary and needs to be read and understood by those doing investigative interviewing or evaluations of sexual abuse. The authors point out that "obtaining accurate testimony about sexual abuse from young children is a complex task. Part of the complexity rests in the fact that there are dangers as well as benefits in the use of leading questioning with children. The benefits are that leading questions are often necessary to elicit information from children about actual events that they have experienced (i.e., genital touching—Goodman); children in the Clarke-Stewart studies appeared more likely to disclose the 'secret' when the interviewer made strong and persistent suggestions. The danger is in children adding erroneous information to their accounts of what had occurred." In both research efforts, we see agreement that children seldom make up facts. The authors summarize that children are most likely to accept an interviewer's suggestions when they are younger, when they are interrogated about an event after a long delay, if they are intimidated by the interviewer, when the interviewer's suggestions are strongly stated and frequently repeated, and when more than one interviewer makes the same strong suggestions.

Goodman and Clarke-Stewart say that "whether children would misconstrue events to the point that an allegation of abuse would result is, based on the authors' research, still debatable. . . . Further research is recommended to address situations that are repeated, personally involving, including imposing frequent and varied interrogations by different authorities, varying the incentives for children to give accurate testimony, and looking for indi-

vidual differences among children that predict heightened
suggestibility and vulnerability."

Goodwin, J. (1991). Problems of belief in the clinical
approach to accounts of victimization. *Journal of
Interpersonal Violence, 6,* 241-245.

This brief commentary points out the need for educat-
ing clinicians regarding the epidemiology of violence and
the use of standard protocols to elicit violence histories
from every patient. Clinicians need to be more aware of
how their own fear of violence may lead to denial. Regarding the veracity of client reports of abuse, Goodwin says
that not "every statement made by every client is a literal
statement about the nature of events." Many factors may
influence the perception and reporting of an event. However, the therapist's job is "to accept the statement and to
join with the client to understand what motivates such a
statement." Goodwin goes on to say that "understanding
what is real, what is partially real, and what is not real will
require of the therapist considerable skill, self-awareness,
and loyalty to sound and client-centered practice skills."

Goodwin, J., Sahd, D., & Rada, R. T. (1978). Incest
hoax: False accusations, false denials. *Bulletin of
the American Academy of Psychiatry and the Law,
6*(3), 269-276.

This 1978 clinical study of false accusations and false
denials points out that actual paternal incest is "fairly

common" in psychiatric patients (the authors give a 5% figure and reference Henderson) and that "incest delusions and hoaxes are probably quite rare." In an early warning about the misuse of null findings, the authors caution that the judgment that an accusation is false should be made positively and not by inference or exclusion.

Gordon, C. (1985). False allegations of abuse in child custody disputes. *New Law Journal*, *135*, 687-689.

Attorney, law professor, and author Gordon recognizes that there are no simple solutions in the complex area of child abuse. He reviews the dramatic increase in child abuse allegations in divorce litigation and says it has in many ways kept pace with increases in child abuse cases in general. He reviews the historical response to allegations being ignored and dismissed as fantasy to the more recent, dangerous potential of "overreacting" and believing that children do not lie. To support his conclusions, he cites the work of Benedek and Schetky, as well as Schuman, work that is not empirically based and is not published in peer reviewed publications. He concludes that "as more information about false allegations of abuse becomes known, the judicial system will develop a reluctance to operate under the assumption that all allegations of abuse are true." Gordon also sees the family court as the ultimate finder of fact with respect to all matters at issue in a custody dispute, including the veracity of allegations of abuse. He goes on to state that the family court should have the role of finding out, by substantial evidence, that the allegations of abuse are true.

Gothard, S. (1989). Backlash, claims and counter-claims in the adjudication of child sexual abuse. *Roundtable Magazine, 1*(1), 12-13.

Gothard, S. (1989). Backlash, claims and counter-claims in the adjudication of child sexual abuse. *Roundtable Magazine, 1*(2), 8-10.

Gothard, S. (1990). Backlash, claims and counter-claims in the adjudication of child sexual abuse. *Roundtable Magazine, 2*(1), 18-20.

In this three-part series, Judge Sol Gothard presents discussion and opinion on a variety of claims and counter-claims regarding the incidence and circumstances of child sexual abuse cases. His opinion is presented in the form of an appellate judgment, and he addresses what has been named the "Battle of the Backlash."

He finds "by a preponderance of the evidence that the claims of child advocates, although presented in good faith, are frequently fraught with exaggeration and, in some cases, misconception. Nonetheless, in general these arguments have the symmetry and truthfulness required to justify judgment in their favor.

"On the other hand, a preponderance of evidence also demonstrates that many claims that have been characterized as the "backlash" also have validity. On balance, however, the backlash has done far more harm than good for the plight of sexually abused children and has contributed to the continued suffering and exploitation of these children."

Green, A. (1988, March). The sex abuse controversy [letter to the editor]. *Journal of the American Academy of Child and Adolescent Psychiatry, 27*, 259.

The author defends his previous article on allegations of sexual abuse occurring in custody or visitation disputes. A recent letter by Dr. Hanson (see Hanson, 1988, in this bibliography) and colleagues took issue with the article for making unsubstantiated claims. Dr. Green points out that the clinical observations made by himself and others were not meant to be hard and fast criteria but rather general guidelines. The concerns of Hanson et al. about the article's potential to mislead the reader should be alleviated by a careful reading. Qualifiers make it clear that the criteria differentiating true and false cases are not consistent and not always present, and that exceptions do occur.

Green, A. (1991). Factors contributing to false allegations of child sexual abuse in custody disputes. *Child & Youth Services, 15*(2), 177-189.

This article describes the underlying psychodynamics of the phenomenon of false allegations of child sexual abuse initiated during child custody disputes. The author states that false accusations are often the result of misin-

terpretation of normal caretaking practices involving
physical or affectionate contact between parent and child
during bathing, toileting, dressing, hugging, or kissing.
Common situations involving false accusations are reviewed, and the impact on the children and families involved is discussed. Factors leading to false accusations
may include a stress-related regression in psychological
functioning, depression, and experience of loss in the
parents following the dissolution of the marriage.

Green, A. H. (1986). True and false allegations of
   sexual abuse in child custody disputes. *Journal of
   the American Academy of Child Psychiatry, 25,*
   449-455.

Targeted to the child psychiatrist, this article states
that more and more wives are making incest allegations
against husbands during custody disputes. One of the ways
Green describes such mothers is as "irate" and with
"prominent paranoid and hysterical psychopathology."
Green presents documentation from 11 cases in his clinical
practice, of which he classifies 4 (36%) as false. Green
offers criteria to differentiate true from false allegations,
among them, statements that sexually abused children
often exhibit fearfulness, inhibition, or seductive behavior
during joint interviews with the father.

Four articles (Corwin et al., 1987; Faller et al., 1991;
Hanson, 1988; and *APSAC Advisor*, Spring, 1991) have
been published that criticize Green's work because of the
small sample size, the prematurity and oversimplication of

the criteria he offers, the reliance on conjoint interviews, and the lack of independent corroboration for the "false" allegation.

Green, A. H. (1991). Factors contributing to false allegations of child sexual abuse in custody disputes. In M. Robin (Ed.), *Assessing child maltreatment reports: The problem of false allegations* (pp. 177-189). Binghamton, NY: Haworth Press.

The author describes several factors that may lead to false allegations of sexual abuse during custody disputes, such as misinterpretation of normal caretaking practices, misinterpretation of common psychological symptoms, and misinterpretation of physical signs and symptoms in the child.

The discussion regarding differentiating between parental sexual overstimulation and actual molestation is confusing. The author offers a case example in which a child is preoccupied "with fellatio and other signs of eroticized behavior, such as frequent masturbation and precocious sexual talk," has made statements about "sucking Daddy's penis," and "gleefully told the evaluator that she touched her father's penis in the shower." The author discusses the parents' sexually permissive lifestyle and then states that this is clearly a case of a child responding to a sexually overstimulating environment rather than a case of true molestation. The basis for this distinction is not explained.

H

Hall, G.C.N. (1989). WAIS-R and MMPI profiles of men who have sexually assaulted children: Evidence of limited utility. *Journal of Personality Assessment, 53,* 404-412.

This article concludes that many perpetrators test as psychologically normal on these tests. The article can be used to effectively challenge testimony that the suspect did not meet the MMPI Pedophile Profile.

Hanson, G. (1988, March). The sex abuse controversy [letter to the editor]. *Journal of the American Academy of Child and Adolescent Psychiatry, 27,* 258-259.

Comments are made on an article by Dr. Arthur Green on allegations of sexual abuse in child custody disputes published in this journal (see Green, 1986). The major concern is that Dr. Green's assertions may be taken as a standard of practice by those relatively inexperienced in the field of sexual abuse and that the article may be used in judicial settings to the detriment of children caught in custody battles who have actually been sexually abused. The author asserts that the evaluation paradigm proposed does not recognize that evaluators often have a very short period of time to make a decision. The author states that Dr. Green's assertions about reactions of the child interviewed in the presence of the abusing parent as indications of abuse are premature and potentially misleading. Hanson concludes that verbalizations of remembered events by children cannot be assumed to be distorted. Other generalizations and the attempt to characterize true and false cases in table form are overly simplistic and may be misleading.

Haynes-Seman, C., & Hart, J. (1988). Assessment evaluation of parent-child relationships in abuse and neglect. In D. C. Bross, R. D. Krugman, M. R. Lenherr, D. A. Rosenberg, & B. D. Schmitt (Eds.), *The new child protection team handbook* (pp. 181-198). New York: Garland.

This chapter describes a videotaped assessment procedure to evaluate parent-child relationships in cases of alleged abuse and neglect. The authors claim that this procedure is useful to reconstruct the child's experiences within a family and to determine the specific psychological conflicts or social factors that resulted in the maltreatment or allegations of maltreatment of the target child. The use of this procedure is based on the authors' belief that "the relationships that have developed in day-to-day interactions, whether healthy or unhealthy, are reflected in the behaviors of both parents and children even when they are aware of being videotaped." The authors also offer an eight-part interview protocol.

In this chapter, the claims made for the usefulness of this interactional assessment procedure are not substantiated with research data.

Haynes-Seman, C., & Krugman, R. (1989). Sexualized attention: Normal interaction or precursor to
sexual abuse? *American Journal of Orthopsychiatry, 59,* 123-142.

This article by two prominent Kempe Center Staff
offers four case studies of videotaped interviews between
children who had been diagnosed with nonorganic failure
to thrive and their parents. The cases had not been referred
for sexual abuse, nor did the Center report the parents for
sexual abuse following the interviews. However, they did
observe a number of infant-parent interactions that they
found to be inappropriately sexualized. They admit that
they do not know whether such interactions are predictive
of sexual abuse, but they note that the parents did seem to
be deriving sexual pleasure from the interactions. They
distinguish this abnormal sexualized attention from normal
parent-child intimacy because of its compulsive, stereo-
typic, repetitive patterning and the absence of normal
infant-parent social exchanges. They speculate that such
sexually stimulating interactions may "contaminate" the
child for normal social experiences and increase the child's
vulnerability to subsequent abuse.

Hewitt, S. K. (1991). Therapeutic management of
    preschool cases of alleged but unsubstantiated
    sexual abuse. *Child Welfare, 70,* 59-67.

This article outlines a step-by-step procedure for
therapeutic management of preschool children considered

at risk as a result of unsubstantiated allegations of sexual abuse, where contact with the alleged offender is being resumed.

The Midwest Children's Resource Center is a specialty child abuse service at Children's Hospital, St. Paul, Minnesota, where, over the past 8 years, seven cases of alleged sexual abuse have used this therapeutic framework. In six cases, there were no additional abuse allegations, and the seventh case involved some questionable behavior but no formal allegations. The purpose of the management approach is outlined clearly as a means of "buying time" for preschool children until their store of information, vocabulary skills, and concepts regarding sexual abuse have expanded sufficiently to allow more accurate reporting if abuse reoccurs.

The plan involves an individual and joint meeting of the case manager/counselor with the child, the nonoffending parent, and the alleged offender. During sessions, specific ground rules are set and clarified for appropriate and inappropriate touching. The child is supported by the counselor, parent, and the alleged offender to report inappropriate touching. Contact between the alleged offender and the child is carefully monitored over time until it expands into comfortable unsupervised visitation. The child's safety is ensured by using the child's demonstrated and verbalized expressions during monitoring sessions to determine the child's perception of his or her degree of safety during visitation. At least 1 year for contact is recommended, with the hope that as these children get older, they can better report and defend themselves in an at-risk situation.

Hlady, L. J., & Gunter, E. J. (1990). Alleged child
abuse in custody access disputes. *Child Abuse &
Neglect, 14,* 591-593.

This article summarizes a study done by the Child
Protective Services Unit at British Columbia Children's
Hospital in Vancouver, British Columbia, Canada, from
January 1 to December 31, 1988. The study examined the
ages, sex, behavior problems, and frequency of positive
physical findings in 370 cases referred to the Unit. In the
study, 11% of the cases involved child custody/access
disputes. Notable findings included the following:

(1) The issue of false allegations of sexual abuse in
custody/access cases is not reflected in the percentage of
physical findings. Corroborative physical findings in the
custody dispute cases were 17.6% and 15% for the noncustody dispute cases.

(2) The need for a disclosure statement in all cases of
child sexual abuse is highlighted by the low incidence of
positive physical evidence of sexual abuse in both custody
and noncustody dispute cases.

(3) A differential was noted in custody dispute versus
nondispute cases involving physical abuse. The 71% positive physical findings in dispute cases versus the 43.6%
positive finding in nondispute cases is thought to be contaminated by the inclusion of cases of neglect, failure-to-
thrive, and high-risk home situations.

The authors emphasize the need for a thorough assessment process in all cases of suspected sexual abuse involving young children and strongly advocate additional

research studies to assist in determining whether or not custody/access disputes are a factor in false allegations.

Horner, T. M., & Guyer, M. J. (1991). Prediction, prevention, and clinical expertise in child custody cases in which allegations of sexual abuse have been made. *Family Law Quarterly, 25,* 217-252.

In this article, Horner and Guyer argue that in ambiguous child custody/abuse cases, experts have no special insights to offer beyond those of the ordinary person. Horner and Guyer compare the current preoccupation with sexual abuse to historical preoccupations with witchcraft and other heresies and argue that "our means of discerning the portents" are no better than were those of the experts during the witchcraft trials.

In their abuse/custody bibliography, they reveal that they use Blush and Ross's SAID (Sex Abuse in Divorce) terminology. Horner and Guyer claim that only 20% of sexual abuse allegations in the context of divorce are substantiated following investigation. They cite Ralph Underwager, Yates, and Musty as sources. They reference the Thoennes and Tjaden studies but mistate the findings because they cite the 2% rate of sexual abuse allegations in contested custody as instigated by mothers against fathers, whereas Thoennes and Tjaden's study shows that only 48% of the total 1.9% figure is by mothers against fathers. Thoennes and Tjaden, the largest study in this area, clearly shows a 50% confirmation rate in these cases, a figure that is consistent with CPS abuse confirmation rates in other kinds of populations. Horner and Guyer cite Green, 1986, but not others, including Faller.

J

Jones, D. (1985). *False reports of child sexual abuse: Do children lie?* Denver, CO: Colorado School of Medicine.

The incidence of false sexual abuse reports and their clinical characteristics were examined in the Denver (Colorado) Department of Social Services. Data for 576 child sexual abuse cases reported in 1983 were used, as well as an additional 38 false cases seen at the C. Henry Kempe National Center. Of the 576 reports, 267 were unfounded, but only a minority of these were false reports. Of the 45 false reports, 6 were made by a child and 38 by an adult. All four of the children making these reports were girls, all suffered from postraumatic stress disorder (PTSD), and all had been victimized in earlier years. Among adults making false reports, PTSD symptoms resulting from childhood victimization were present in some, and two showed psychotic illness. Similarly, in the second sample, children making accusations were preponderantly girls, with most showing PTSD symptoms related to prior victimization. Adults making false accusations generally were involved in acrimonious custody disputes, and most exhibited PTSD related to their own childhood victimization.

Jones, D. P., & McGraw, J. M. (1987). Reliable and fictitious accounts of sexual abuse to children. *Journal of Interpersonal Violence, 2,* 27-45.

Jones and McGraw reviewed almost 600 reports of sexual abuse made to Denver Protective Services in a single year. They found the rate of false allegations below 10% but noted that the majority of allegations determined to be false arose in divorce situations. Jones and Seig followed up in a subsequent study (1988) of 20 divorce/ abuse cases and found a false allegation rate of 20% (four cases), none of which was determined to be a deliberate fabrication.

Jones, D., & Seig, A. (1988). Child sexual abuse allegations in custody or visitation cases: A report of 20 Cases. In E. B. Nicholson, & J. Bulkley (Eds.), *Sexual abuse allegations in custody and visitation cases* (pp. 22-36). Washington, DC: American Bar Association.

This chapter examines the characteristics of a small sample of 20 cases evaluated at the C. Henry Kempe Center, where child sexual abuse allegations and a parental custody dispute coexisted. Methods of clinical evaluation included review of prior materials, interviews with the child and current caregivers, and interviews with the child in the company of the alleged abuser. Results reported information in the following areas: clinical validation, who made the report, vindictiveness between adults, emotional disturbance in the accuser, abnormal parent/child relationships, emotional disturbance in the perpetrator, timing of allegation, the child's emotional state, physical evidence, confessions, polygraph tests, and type of court in which the cases were heard. In the four cases that were found to be fictitious, no criminal charges were filed against those accused. An appendix gives supplementary methods of clinical evaluation.

K

Kaplan, S., & Kaplan, S. (1981). The child's accusation of sexual abuse during a divorce and custody struggle. *Hillside Journal of Clinical Psychiatry, 3*, 81-95.

This article warns that sexual abuse allegations in the context of divorce may be false. The authors describe one case in detail and allude to another. In the primary case described, the older child (a boy) recanted the abuse when "stressed" by the skeptical therapist in a joint interview with the alleged offenders. The authors attribute these "false" allegations to brainwashing and folie a deux in the mother's family but offer no clinical evidence in support of these hypotheses. This single case study is often cited as evidence of a growing incidence of false sexual abuse allegations.

Kendall-Tackett, K. (1991). Believing children vs. being neutral: What you think can influence your judgments about suspected victims of sexual abuse. *APSAC Advisor*, 4(3), 4.

This study of 201 Boston-area professionals correlated expectations about believing children with perceptions of children's behavior with anatomical dolls. Those who tend to believe children found indicators of possible abuse with these dolls more convincing than did those whose attitude was neutral. The authors point out that the study does not show which attitude led to more accurate judgments. However, professionals' expectations did not correlate with the number of false reports in their caseloads, a result that is inconsistent with Everson and Boat's 1989 and 1992 studies.

Lloyd, D. (Ed.). (1990). *Allegations of child sexual abuse in custody and visitation situations: Proceedings of a think tank.* Huntsville, AL: National Children's Advocacy Center.

Supported by the National Center on Child Abuse & Neglect, Bud Cramer and Howard Pohl, attorneys at law, moderated a think tank in March 1989 that included Lowrance, Bulkley, Froning, Salter, Bunk, Corwin,

Ducote, Pence, Plum, Brogna, Berg, King, Saunders, and Kinney as participants. There was discussion by participants on the following issues: validity of the allegations (validation criteria), possible bias against women being vindictive Moms in raising these concerns, issues of coaching and the need for prosecution to prove indoctrination, jurisdictional conflict or overlap between court systems and investigations, and the need for education and innovative techniques of arbitration and medication.

Loftus, E. (1992). The malleability of memory. *APSAC Advisor*, *5*(3), 7-9.

This article is an excerpt from the author's book, *Witness for the Defense*. It describes the author's expert testimony for the defense in a case where a camp counselor was accused of molestation. The author states that this case involved the mother of a 5-year-old girl who became alarmed when she heard her daughter repeating slang terms for the male sex organ. She began to question her daughter repeatedly regarding whether the counselor had touched her. At first the child said no, but after two weeks of the mother's questions, the child said that he had. Dr. Loftus testified at the camp counselor's trial regarding studies demonstrating that children can be led into remembering something that did not happen if it is suggested to them. The defendant was found not guilty.

M

MacFarlane, K., & White, S. (1990). Point/counter-point: Should alleged child sexual abuse victims be reinforced in forensic interviews? *Violence UpDate, 1*(4), pp. 6-7.

MacFarlane and White state that there have been a number of recent court cases in which the issue of whether or not a child's disclosure was influenced by the interviewer's behavior has been a focal point. These two experts debate whether reinforcing the statements of a child sexual abuse victim contaminates the interview.

MacFarlane states that "the only relevant research in this area actually contradicts the premise that positive reinforcement leads to inaccuracy. . . . If we propose to tailor forensic interview techniques in response to unsupported defense claims, let us at least find out what may be at stake for child victims in this trade-off. Are we so willing to let legal prerogatives dictate the future directions of clinical intervention in this field? Could we be exchanging good clinical practice for forensic acceptability?" White, on the other hand, states that "it is well known that reinforcers can be used to entice, coerce, and otherwise manipulate what the child may be offering to the interviewer. Until we know just what level of reinforcement has a distorting effect on disclosure, interviewers . . . should refrain from utilizing such techniques in forensic interviews. The question being addressed here is whether these reinforcers have a place in legally sensitive interviews with children as the clients."

McAnulty, R. D., & Adams, H. E. (1990). Patterns of sexual arousal of accused child molesters involved in custody disputes. *Archives of Sexual Behavior, 19,* 541-556.

The authors used penile plethysmography to examine sexual preferences in a sample of men accused of child molestation. Half of the sample had been accused during the course of a divorce and custody dispute, while the other half had been accused in other contexts. The results indicated that 46% of the custody dispute subjects and 67% of the noncustody dispute subjects exhibited deviant arousal (defined as greater arousal to child stimuli than to adult stimuli).

McGough, L. S. (1991). Commentary: Assessing the credibility of witnesses' statements. In J. Doris (Ed.), *The suggestibility of children's recollections* (pp. 165-167). Washington, DC: American Psychological Association.

This chapter is a commentary on Raskin and Esplin's chapter on Criteria-Based Content Analysis (CBCA) that appears in the same volume. An annotation of Raskin and Esplin's chapter appears in this bibliography (see Raskin & Esplin, 1991). McGough observes that the CBCA is an instrument designed to assist the expert witness in assessing the credibility of a witness's statement. Noting that this technique was developed in Europe, where expert testimony on witness credibility is accepted, McGough comments on the claims of CBCA within the context of the American legal system.

McGough explains that in the Anglo-American legal system, most "courts have received expert testimony explaining the special behaviors of children who are sexual abuse victims as a class or group" but states that "only a handful of courts would now permit any expert to go one step further and testify whether a particular child victim's statement is reliable or not." She goes on to say that "in the Anglo-American legal system, witness credibility is a question of fact to be determined by the jury or, in most cases, by the court alone."

McGough suggests two alternative ways of utilizing information from the CBCA. She suggests that trained experts using this technique "can be very helpful to prosecutors (or counsel in civil cases) in determining whether to go forward with a case pivoting on a child's allegations." She further suggests that "the methodology could be very helpful in properly training those who interview children." For another commentary on the Raskin and Esplin chapter, see Wells and Loftus, 1991.

McGovern, K. B. (1991). Was there really child sexual abuse or is there another explanation. In M. Robin (Ed)., *Assessing child maltreatment reports: The problem of false allegations* (pp. 115-127). Binghamton, NY: Haworth Press.

This chapter discusses the diagnostic errors that may occur during the interdisciplinary evaluation of child sexual abuse allegations. The authors point out unintentional human errors that law enforcement, social services, medical, and mental health professionals may make during child sexual abuse investigations. Errors by law enforcement and social services personnel include failing to provide long-term and comprehensive evaluations and ignoring fundamental principles of child psychology. Medical personnel do not routinely examine the genitals of little girls unless there has been a specific complaint. Mental health professionals can be misinformed about initial child sexual abuse allegations by an adult providing a distorted analysis of what really occurred or by a child influenced by a variety of suggestive and contaminating factors. Suggestions for avoiding the problems that these groups of professionals may encounter are offered.

McGraw, M. J., & Smith, H. A. (1992). Child sexual abuse allegations amidst divorce and custody proceedings: Refining the validation process. *Journal of Child Sexual Abuse, 1*, 49-62.

This article analyzes 18 cases investigated by the Boulder County (Colorado) Sexual Abuse Team from March, 1986, through July, 1987. The authors state that "determining whether such allegations are reliable or fictitious presents a challenge to caseworkers who are apt to find themselves caught up in the highly charged atmosphere of divorce and custody proceedings." Out of the 290 cases then investigated, these 18 constituted all the sexual abuse cases that involved a contested custody dispute. Initially, only 5.6% of these cases (N = 1) had been founded, and 94.4% were considered unfounded reports (N = 17). After the authors applied the clinical process of validation used at the Kempe Center in Denver, Colorado, the cases were subject to further review and categorized as reliable accounts, recantations, unsubstantiated suspicions, insufficient information, fictitious reports by adults, and fictitious reports by children. Subsequent to applying this clinical process of validation, the number of cases categorized as founded increased to 44.4% (N = 8). Of the remaining 55.6%, there were five cases of unsubstantiated suspicion, two of insufficient information, two fictitious reports from adults, and one fictitious report from a child.

In their discussion, McGraw and Smith observe that the revised founded rate of 44.4% is only slightly lower than substantiation rates found in sexual abuse cases reported to child protective services overall, whether or not in the context of custody disputes; they cite the 1986 study by Thoennes, Cosby, and Pearson of all cases that had a 50% substantiation rate. They explain the very low rate of initial founding of such cases by the Boulder Sexual Abuse Team as due in part to the impact of divorce/custody proceedings on the objectivity of clinicians.

Morris, S. (1988, August 1). From marital ruins, un-
thinkable torment for young innocents. *Legal
Times*, pp. 16-17.

This attorney speaks to the perceived increase in child
sexual abuse cases in the context of divorce/custody litigation having been compared to the climate surrounding the
Salem Witch Trials in 1692. She asks if we are on another
witch hunt. An overwhelming body of scientific investigation and literature suggests the answer is no. The author
discusses the supposed explosion in child abuse allegations
and their possible fabrications. She goes on to say, from
her own client research and other recent studies, that she
has found that divorcing mothers who say their husbands
are sexually abusing their children are women with independence of mind or backbone, not likely to stay quiet
about such things. When concerns about witch hunts or
other frivolity are put aside, the central issue in her mind
in divorce/custody/abuse litigation becomes how evidence
can be elicited while causing a minimal amount of trauma
to the child, at the same time maintaining the accused rights
to confrontation and putting before the trier of fact only
legally admissible evidence.

The author discusses the difficulties for two 6-year-
old cases: issues of fantasy, memory, coaching, language
in interviewing, credibility, child testimony, anatomical
dolls, and "Kelly-Fryee." She presents a survey of the field
regarding child witness expectations. She predicts children
will have to testify more frequently to add clarity and
recognizes the eyes upon the court and how these cases are
handled.

Morris, S. J. (1989). Sexually abused children of divorce. *Journal of the American Academy of Matrimonial Lawyers, 5,* 27-46.

In this article, Morris quotes the Association and Conciliation Courts study (Thoennes & Tjaden) that sex abuse allegation rates, at 2% of contested custody cases, are far smaller than current media reports would indicate. She notes that in its most recent form, the backlash focuses on sexual abuse reporting, evaluation, and processing through the courts and that most experts believe fabrication to be very infrequent.

Morris presents data from 8 custody abuse cases in her practice, using the MMPI. Like Faller, Morris points out that allegations of ongoing abuse may first surface during divorce and may be likely to be believed, partly because the perpetrator may now have diminished opportunity to prevent disclosure. In addition, Morris agrees with Faller that the stresses of divorce may precipitate abuse. Morris's sample of 8 contained 2 cases of incest that had begun before separation. In the other 6 cases, the male abuser had opposed the marital separation (among Faller's 1990 larger sample of fathers who began abuse during visits, three quarters had opposed the divorce). Morris also found that in her sample, postdivorce incest assaults were more painful and injurious than those she has seen in intact families. Sample size, however, was very small and not random.

Morris cites Goodman's work on the often unjustified skepticism of jurors toward child witnesses. She also comments on the use of anatomical dolls and concludes, "No

well-designed, large studies document that dolls put forth
sexual behavior that the children have not observed or
experienced. . . . Normal children . . . do not repetitively
perform acts with the dolls as do the sexually abused
children; they do not express aggression with the dolls, nor
do they repeatedly press the genitals with their hands as do
the abused children. They explore once and then are no
longer interested."

Myers, J.E.B. (1989-90). Allegations of child sexual
   abuse in custody and visitation litigation: Recommendations for improved fact finding and child
   protection. *Journal of Family Law*, *28*, 1-41.

This article provides a broad overview of the legal,
psychological, and social issues that affect the resolution
of child custody cases with sexual abuse allegations. The
issue of fabricated allegations is discussed in detail. The
author reviews recent research and concludes that the
evidence suggests that only a small proportion of sexual
abuse allegations appear to be fabricated. The article points
out the complexities involved in distinguishing among
true, misperceived, and fabricated allegations. The article
discusses evidentiary and constitutional issues such as the
admissibility of children's testimony in legal proceedings
and constraints regarding the use of expert testimony.
Recommendations are offered for improving communication between family court and child protective services and
between family court and juvenile court. It is suggested that
it is best if psychological evaluations are conducted by

court-appointed mental health professionals in order to avoid parties shopping for hired guns.

Myers, J.E.B., Bays, J., Becker, J., Berliner, L., Corwin, D., & Saywitz, K. (1989). Expert testimony in child sexual abuse litigation. *Nebraska Law Review*, *68*, 1-145.

This entire journal issue is devoted to this article that summarizes the current state of knowledge, theory, and research regarding the victims and perpetrators of child sexual abuse. The article focuses on expert testimony in the courtroom as it relates to these issues.

N

Nicholson, E. B. (1988). Child sexual abuse allegations in family court proceedings: A survey of legal issues. In E. B. Nicholson & J. Bulkley (Eds.), *Sexual abuse allegations in custody and visitation cases* (pp. 255-277). Washington, DC: American Bar Association.

This article describes how child sexual abuse allegations may affect the legal context of custody and visitation decisions. The family court's limited legal authority and limited resources make it difficult for the family court to adequately respond in child sexual abuse cases. The role of the court in supervising visitation when any form of sexual abuse has occurred needs to be better defined. The need for protective mechanisms in family court proceedings will probably increase. Protective mechanisms found in the juvenile court, such as mandatory appointment of guardians ad litem, might also be adopted by family courts. Case management and planning will help the family court best serve its responsibility for the child.

Nicholson, E. B., & Bulkley, J. (Eds.). (1988). *Sexual abuse allegations in custody and visitation cases.* Washington, DC: American Bar Association.

This book examines sexual abuse allegations in custody and visitation cases. Bringing together some of the most recent work from the many disciplines involved in the field, this book is roughly divided into materials discussing emerging policy issues and background. There is an overview of the problem followed by a look at false allegations. Investigations and evaluations of child sexual abuse cases arising in a custody or visitation context are described. The court process is studied critically, with recommendations for improvements in procedures for children. Background readings excerpted or reprinted from other sources are included.

P

Paradise, J., Rostain, A., & Nathanson, M. (1988). Substantiation of sexual abuse charges when parents dispute custody visitation. *Pediatrics*, *81*, 835-839.

Sexual abuse cases in a hospital-based consecutive series and in a clinical practice were reviewed. Abuse allegations with and without a concomitant custody or visitation dispute were compared. A custody or visitation dispute occurred in 12 of 31 sexual abuse complaints lodged against a parent. Allegedly abused children whose parents contested custody or visitation were significantly younger than those for whom custody or visitation was not an issue (5.4 vs. 7.8 years). Sexual abuse allegations were substantiated less frequently when there was concomitant parental conflict (67% vs. 95% nonsignificant) but were nevertheless substantiated more than half of the time.

Pearson, J., & Thoennes, N. (1990). Custody after divorce: Demographic and attitudinal patterns. *American Journal of Orthopsychiatry*, *60*, 233-249.

In this reanalysis of data from a large sample of divorced parents originally seen in a number of different studies, joint residential custody was found to be favorable for couples who chose this arrangement and for their children. The article does not provide data about couples who were forced into joint custody over the objections of one parent. Children's adjustment appeared to be unrelated to custody type.

Perry, N. W. (1992). How children remember and why they forget. *APSAC Advisor*, *5*(3), 1-16.

This article reviews the development of children's memory and discusses the impact of stress, intimidation, and inducements to keep secrets and suggestions on the accuracy of their recollections. Some of the conclusions are that children are capable of accurate memory of simple events but may have difficulty conceptualizing complex events. Stressful events that involve intimidation seem to be remembered less well, while children's memories are better for stressful events not involving intimidation. In general, children seem to have better recall in familiar situations. Children have a less sophisticated ability to use memory strategies when compared to adults, but nonetheless, "on some tasks young children perform as well as, or better, than adults." Some studies have found children are no more suggestible than adults while others find that in certain circumstances children are more suggestible.

Quinn, K. M. (1988). The credibility of children's allegations of sexual abuse. *Behavioral Sciences and the Law, 6,* 181-199.

This article provides a thorough review of the complexities involved in assessing children's allegations of sexual abuse. The article reviews current estimates of false positive rates and points out that professional biases have led to both false positive and false negative assessments.

There is a review of research on factors that affect children's credibility, such as characteristics of memory, children's suggestibility, and developmental limitations in the areas of language and cognition. Some of the dynamics of sexual abuse that have an impact on how credible an allegation may appear are discussed. These include delayed disclosure, recantation, simulated intercourse, and the frequency of children having positive feelings toward the perpetrator. The author also discusses dissociative and posttraumatic stress symptoms that may result in victims appearing less credible.

Suggestions for validation procedures are made. Maintaining independence or neutrality is presented as a key issue. It is recommended that evaluators use multiple interviews, take thorough psychosocial histories, and examine the detail and emotion in sexual abuse disclosures. The author also points out the importance of assessing any possible motivation for making a false complaint. The clinical presentations of several common types of false complaints are reviewed.

Quinn, K. M. (1991). False and unsubstantiated sexual abuse allegations: Clinical issues. In M. Robin (Ed.), *Assessing child maltreatment reports: The problem of false allegations* (pp. 145-157). Binghamton, NY: Haworth Press.

The author discusses the historical, societal, legal, and psychological causes that contribute to the trends of underreporting and overreporting of child sexual abuse allegations and to evaluations that come up with false negative or false positive conclusions. Several explanations for false allegations are offered, such as an overanxious child or parent; alterations in family practices concerning privacy, nudity, toileting, or bathing, or changes in perceptions of these practices in separating or divorcing families; the intentional production of false or grossly exaggerated physical or psychological symptoms to achieve goals such as alternate placement or custody; the copycat phenomenon; and the overinterpretation of interview data. The reasons true allegations may be dismissed as false are presented, including the lack of corroborating evidence in cases where a child cannot or will not talk about the abuse, the lack of understanding on the part of professionals concerning the natural history of abuse, the failure to report abuse, and the lack of preparation or the overpreparation of child witnesses.

R

Raskin, D. C., & Esplin, P. W. (1991). Assessment of children's statements of sexual abuse. In J. Doris (Ed.), *The suggestibility of children's recollections* (pp. 153-165). Washington, DC: American Psychological Association.

This chapter discusses the Criteria-Based Content Analysis (CBCA) and reviews two studies on the reliability and validity of this technique. CBCA is a technique designed to assess the validity of a witness's statement and to distinguish between statements about an event that was actually experienced and statements that are fabricated. This technique is based on a statement reality analysis originally developed by Undeutsch in Germany in the 1950s and further elaborated "over decades of application in tens of thousands of sexual abuse cases in Germany." (For more information on the Statement Validity Analysis, also taken from Undeutsch's work, see Yulle (1988) in this bibliography.)

In order to apply the CBCA, children's tape recorded and transcribed disclosures about an event are analyzed according to 19 specific content criteria, such as the logical structure, quantity of details, contextual embedding, and reproduction of conversations. The authors acknowledge that the technique has only recently been subjected to studies of its reliability and validity, and this chapter reports on two of the first such studies.

The first validation study involved asking 98 school children to produce two stories, one about a real event and one about a made-up event. The children were given specific categories of events to use in their stories, such as medical procedures, accidents, or animal attacks. Significant differences between stories about real and imagined events were found only for stories about medical events.

The second study reported in this chapter analyzes the disclosures of sexual abuse victimization made by 20 children in "confirmed" cases and compares them to the statements of 20 children in "doubtful" cases. Cases defined as confirmed involved either a perpetrator confession or physical evidence. Cases that were termed doubtful were those lacking confessions or physical evidence and where there had not been a successful prosecution. The study found that the confirmed cases had significantly higher scores on the content criterion. The authors conclude that the results of these studies "lend strong support to the underlying principles and hypotheses of CBCA." Commentaries on the Raskin and Esplin chapter appear in the same volume and are annotated in this bibliography (see Wells & Loftus, 1991, and McGough, 1991).

Remley, T., & Miranti, J. (1991). Child custody evaluator: A new role for mental health counselors. *Journal of Mental Health Counseling, 13*(3), 334-342.

This is an excellent basic overview for mental health counselors interested in serving as independent child custody evaluators. The article covers the recommended areas of expertise: the importance of impartiality, including the risks of agreeing to evaluate only one party; how to market the service; how to conduct a professional process involving fees and court contacts; guidelines for a standardized protocol; how to write a professional report; the risks and challenges of court testimony; and finally, the rewards of the evaluator role.

Robin, M. (1991). The social construction of child abuse and false allegations. In M. Robin (Ed.), *Assessing child maltreatment reports: The problem of false allegations* (pp. 1-34). Binghamton, NY: Haworth Press.

Focusing on the work of C. Henry Kempe, the evolution and development of awareness of child abuse and neglect as a serious problem are discussed. The social organization of child protection services and the role of child protection professionals in shaping professional and public attitudes about the nature of the problem are examined. The moral panic created by statistics concerning the high incidence of child abuse is discussed and issues of underreporting and overreporting of abuse are addressed. The chapter focuses on examples of false allegation cases, studies of false allegations, and false allegations in divorce and custody dispute cases. In addition, the social stigma assigned to a person reported for child abuse and the impact of false allegations are reviewed.

Rogers, M. (1990). Delusional disorder and the evolution of mistaken sexual allegations in child
custody cases. *American Journal of Forensic Psychology*, *10*, 47-69.

Forensic psychologist Martha Rogers discusses the
characteristics of five cases of alleged sexual molestation
by a parent referred to her private practice for child custody
evaluations. In all of these cases, the molestation was
believed not to have occurred. The author cautions that
before making a diagnosis of delusional disorder in the
alleging parent, the examiner must look carefully at all
aspects of the allegation to make a determination regarding
the likelihood that the abuse occurred. An argument is
made that there should be very thorough assessments conducted in these cases, including, in some cases, a second
opinion psychiatric evaluation. Psychological testing is not
seen as contributing much to the diagnosis. A thorough,
detailed interview with the alleging parent should be docu-
mented on audio or video tape or with detailed notes. It is
suggested that "the report of the situation in which the
delusional patient infers that molestation has first occurred
will be qualitatively different than that seen in actual cases
of child molestation." The implications for child custody
assessments are discussed, and it is suggested that it may
harm a child's emotional development to remain in the care
of a parent who persistently pressures them to accept a
delusional belief.

Romero, S. (1990). Child sexual abuse in custody and visitation disputes: Problems, progress, and prospects. *Golden Gate University Law Review*, *20*, 647-680.

This article points out that, although it is often assumed that an allegation of sexual abuse arising in a divorce proceeding is false, data from the most comprehensive studies using large samples find that few involve deliberately fabricated allegations.

The article discusses the investigation and assessment of sexual abuse allegations with an eye toward how such evidence is seen in court. It goes over children's testimony and then reviews issues related to expert testimony. It explains that the admissibility of expert witness testimony may depend on whether the court characterizes it as "expert opinion" or as "scientific" evidence (which must meet the Kelly-Frye Test). The use of diagnostic tools, such as the Child Sexual Abuse Accommodation Syndrome and anatomical dolls, are discussed in this light. The article compares appellate decisions in New York and California and points out that New York has tended to consider a mental health professional's testimony as expert opinion, while California has tended to consider the information as scientific evidence, requiring it to meet the more stringent Kelly-Frye Test (which often results in the evidence being inadmissible). The article points out that, on the other hand, courts tend to accept medical expert opinion without testing it as scientific evidence.

The article also discusses case management and the jurisdiction of family and dependency court. It refers to and endorses the California Child Victim Witness Judicial Advisory Committee Final Report's recommendation that a family relations division be created to handle both dependency and civil family law matters.

S

Salter, A. C. (1988). *Treating child sex offenders and victims.* Newbury Park, CA: Sage.

This well-researched and clearly argued book is one of the best for understanding perpetrators. It also provides a critique and discussion of family systems theory, humanistic psychology, and Parents United, and proposes treatment strategies for sex offenders. The appendixes contain many useful assessment instruments.

Saywitz, K., & Damon, L. (1988). Developmental considerations for interviewers. In MacFarlane, K., & Feldmeth, J. (Eds.), *Response to child sexual abuse: The clinical interview* (pp. 5-10). New York: Guilford.

This article points out four principles for understanding how children think, relate, and communicate differently from adults. First: Children create their own explanations for how the world operates. Second: Children go through predictable phases in development. Third: There is a great deal of individual difference in the rate at which different children develop skills. And fourth: Different skills develop separately and at different rates for any given child.

In order to use these principles to develop appropriate interview techniques, the interviewer would first observe and interact with the child in certain structured activities specifically designed to assess the child's developmental level and unique ways of understanding the world in key areas such as sense of time, number concepts, language development, personal descriptions, causality, and understanding the perspective of others.

Saywitz, K., & Damon, L. (1988). Honesty, memory, and sexual knowledge. In MacFarlane, K., & Feldmeth, J. (Eds.), *Response to child sexual abuse: The clinical interview* (pp. 11-14). New York: Guilford.

The authors recognize the necessity of knowing what to expect from a child under the age of 7 in terms of honesty, memory capacity, and sexual knowledge as particularly important in interviewing about possible sexual abuse. Regarding honesty, do children lie? Researchers have failed to find a correlation between age and honest behavior. It does not appear that we grow more honest as we grow older, the authors summarize. They suggest interviewers might be better off to ask young children to promise to tell what *really* happened versus abstract questions about differences between truths and lies. Very young children may not understand what the word "differences" means.

Regarding memory, do children remember as well as adults do? The authors point out that children's memories are not necessarily inferior to the memories of adults. The errors made by children tend to be errors of omission rather than commission. The authors state that "children, like adults, are more accurate about core, central events than about peripheral details. They are more accurate about familiar, salient, and personally meaningful encounters than about events they perceive to be unimportant and unfamiliar." Thus, sexual abuse is more apt to be remembered accurately. The authors go on to discuss children's understanding of reproduction, their knowledge about sexual activities, their knowledge of sexual differences, children's drawings, and sexuality, and their sexualized behaviors.

The authors, in conclusion, say that "being interviewed about sexual molestation requires that children honestly report memories of past events of a sexual nature. Kids bring both strengths and limitations to the interview situation. The interviewer must be aware of this when assessing honesty, memory capability, and age-appropriate sexual knowledge and activity. Keeping these developmental considerations at hand will help the interviewer or evaluator make decisions regarding reporting and custody."

Saywitz, K., Goodman, G. S., Nicholas, E., & Moan, S. (1990). Children's memories of genital examinations: Implications for cases of child sexual assault. *Journal of Consulting and Clinical Psychology*, 59, 682-691.

Seventy-two healthy 5- and 7-year-old girls participated in this study in which they received a standard medical checkup. For half of the girls, this included an external anal/genital examination, and for half it did not. One week or one month later, the children were asked to recall what happened, to reenact the checkup with anatomically correct dolls, and to answer specific and misleading questions.

The majority of those who received genital and anal touching failed to report it during open-ended interviews. They disclosed only in response to specific questions. When asked directly, children in the nongenital condition never falsely reported genital touch in free recall or doll demonstration; the false report rate was low. The authors found that only in the nongenital condition were there significant age differences in free recall and doll demonstrations. This implicated socioemotional factors as suppressing the reports of older children who did experience genital contact.

Saywitz, K. J. (1992). Enhancing children's memory with the cognitive interview. *APSAC Advisor*, 5(3), pp. 9-10.

This article discusses the modification of the "cognitive interview," originally developed as an aid in forensic interviews of adult crime victims, for use with children. The technique, which has been shown to elicit 35% to 58% more information from adults, involves a guided memory search that asks the individual to mentally reconstruct the environmental and personal context, to report every detail that comes to mind, in any order, and to report the events from a variety of perspectives. Once the instructions were made appropriate for children, the technique was tested against the standard police interview in two studies with school-age children. The first study found that the cognitive interview elicited 26% more accurate information. The second study, which allowed the children more opportunity to rehearse the technique, found an increase of 45% in accurate information recalled.

Saywitz, K. J., Goodman, G. S., & Myers, J.E.B. (1990). Can children provide accurate eyewitness reports? *Violence UpDate*, *1*(1), pp. 1-3.

This is a summary of the Saywitz and Goodman research that a judge might be likely to read because it is brief and clear. Like all of their research, it indicates that children are better witnesses, and less suggestible, than most of the public (juries) and professionals (CPS workers, expert witnesses, judges) believe them to be. These researchers consistently find that children ages 10 or 11 are no more suggestible than adults, children ages 4-9 are sometimes more suggestible, and 3-year-olds may be par-

ticularly subject to the influence of suggestion. Resistance
to suggestion appears to be highest concerning core aspects
of actually experienced, salient events. Although children
can lie, they seem to do so primarily to avoid punishment.
The authors conclude that there is no solid, scientific
evidence to date that children confuse fantasy and reality
and that they invent charges of sexual abuse.

Schaefer, M., & Guyer, M. (1988, August). *Allegations
of sexual abuse in custody and visitation disputes: A
legal and clinical challenge.* Paper presented at 96th
Annual Conference of the American Psychological
Association, Atlanta, GA.

This paper deals only with false allegations in the
context of divorce and does not alert clinicians to issues
connected with actual cases of sexual abuse in such situations. Schaefer and Guyer cite Benedek, Schetky, Blush,
Ross, and Green in support of their opening statement that
sexual abuse allegations arise frequently in divorce/cus-
tody situations. All the claims made in the references they
cite were based on clinical impressions alone and not on
statistical data.

Schaefer and Guyer examine a subset of sexual abuse
allegations that have three characteristics: They are "often
quite vague," they occur in the context of custody or
visitation disputes, and they involve very young children.
They note that each one of these characteristics makes
determinations of truth or falsity problematic. Although
they observe that deliberate fabrications are rare in their

experience, they focus on the likelihood that such allegations may be false in a number of other ways. The parent
may perceive any sexualized behavior by the child as
evidence of abuse, interpret the common behaviors of
preschoolers reacting to divorce as symptoms of abuse, or
mistake routine parental behavior with children, such as
the application of genital ointments or normal roughhous-
ing, for sexual abuse.

Finally Schaefer and Guyer state that the "intense
narcissistic rage" that some parents experience following
separation may drive a parent to pursue abuse allegations
because of hatred, distrust, and a desire to hurt the other
parent. The authors refer to those persistent efforts in this
latter category that lead to repeated evaluations as similar
to "Munchhausen's by Proxy." They seem to classify such
cases as mistaken or false allegations rather than as deliberate fabrications.

The authors call for thorough evaluations of the alleging spouse as well as of the alleged perpetrator. They offer
an "emerging" psychological profile of such the parent
allegedly making the allegation, which includes compro-
mised reality testing because of strong affect, rage, obses-
sive rumination about the ex-spouse's sexual behavior, and
a "somewhat paranoid" view of themselves as the child's
sole protector. They call for maintenance or restoration of
the relationship between the child and the alleged perpetrator while the evaluation is proceeding. They offer no
warnings about the physical and psychological risks to a
child of fostering such a continuing relationship where
actual sexual abuse or assault has taken place or may again
take place in the absence of supervision.

The authors also discuss other issues, such as children's memories, their suggestibility, and the use of anatomical dolls.

Schetky, D. (1986). Editorial: Emerging issues in child sexual abuse. *Journal of the American Academy of Child Psychiatry, 25,* 490-492.

Schetky introduces a 1986 issue on child sexual abuse by citing 1984 Humane Society statistics to show that 58% of child sexual abuse allegations remain unsubstantiated. She describes the "parallel and related" development of increased sexual abuse allegations in custody litigations, describing such an allegation as a "surefire way of getting the court's attention" in order to suspend visitation and "expunge a former spouse from one's life." She warns that as the "psychodynamics" of these cases become complex, we must consider both false allegations and false retractions. She then introduces the articles in the special issue, of which the one by Green has been the best known and is reviewed in this bibliography.

Schudson, C. (1992). Antagonistic parents in family courts: False allegations or false assumptions about true allegations of child sexual abuse? *Journal of Child Sexual Abuse, 1,* 111-114.

Judge Schudson, in the first of three commentaries on this subject (see Bross and Toth), recognizes that child sexual abuse allegations in family law court battles may be viewed on the surface more skeptically than those found in juvenile or criminal court for one or two valid reasons. A vengeful parent may regard the allegation as a way to seek advantage in the dispute or as a method of spousal harassment. Also, a false allegation can enter family court without passing through investigation and review by system professionals who typically screen juvenile and criminal cases.

Family law court judges may be even less informed than their juvenile and criminal court colleagues because of the lack of such screening and the information from that process. If the family court judges hold prevalent misconceptions about children, they may deny themselves the chance to evaluate important evidence. An example of a highly publicized case is Dr. Elizabeth Morgan, who maintained that the judge failed to reach the correct decision largely because he denied himself the opportunity to consider essential evidence. The author cites the Federal Court of Appeals reversal of the trial judge's decision and why.

Schudson points out that, contrary to what many may assume, false allegations remain relatively rare in family law courts. Allegations of abuse occur in about 2% of these kinds of disputes and most of those are substantiated (see Thoennes and Pearson). He notes that apparently even the most antagonistic parents do not allege child sexual abuse. He predicts that family court judges will be seeing an increasing number of sexual abuse allegations resulting primarily from increasing disclosures of real abuse.

Finally, Judge Schudson appeals to the need for understanding that all allegations of child sexual abuse must be evaluated in a thorough and sensitive manner to separate the few allegations that are false from the many that are true, particularly in dealing with antagonistic parents disputing custody/visitation.

Schuman, D. (1986). False accusations of physical and sexual abuse. *Bulletin of the American Academy of Psychiatry and the Law, 14*(1), pp. 5-21.

This article discusses 7 cases from a psychiatrist's practice in which reported physical and/or sexual abuse claims were shown to be nonvalid. The author states that child sexual abuse is sometimes mistakenly overreported; this article focuses on one potential area that can generate a substantial segment of false positives: conflicted domestic relationships in litigation. Such situations generate striking, regressive affect and behavior, especially when issues of child custody or visitation erupt. Parental regression has been discussed in the literature, but children regress also: Behavioral symptoms erupt with negative and social disruptions, and instinctual material regarding both sex and anger is more accessible to consciousness than is age-appropriate. The author feels that heightened instinctual forces in children and regressive loosening of prelitigation character defenses in adults, both in the context of stressful family breakdown, combine to generate genuine perceptions of abuse but invalid reports. This study is based, however, on a small clinical sample with a lack of any independent confirmation that the allegations were false.

Schuman, D. C. (1989). False accusations of physical and sexual abuse cases. *Connections*, *3*(4), pp. 6-10.

Schuman cites 7 cases from his Massachusetts forensic practice that he and the court determined to be false. The summary of his observations are reflected in his conclusions in the article in the *Bulletin of the American Academy of Psychiatry and the Law*, 1986 (see Schuman, 1986, annotation).

Scott, R. L., & Stone, D. A. (1986). MMPI profile constellations in incest families. *Journal of Consulting and Clinical Psychology*, *54*, 364-368.

These researchers looked at MMPI profiles for family members who were in treatment for incest related issues. Testing was done on the perpetrators, who consisted of 33 natural fathers and 29 stepfathers, as well as on 44 nonoffending mothers and 22 daughters who had been the victims of the abuse. The subjects were compared to 128 matched controls in the four corresponding categories. The daughters demonstrated significantly more pathology than the adults and the control group, with elevations on the F, Pt, and Sc scales. The study found no significant pathology in either group of perpetrators, and the authors point out that "this finding is consistent with clinical literature that speculates that mental illness will be found in only a small minority of cases." This can be a useful resource when psychological testing is being used to determine validity of an allegation of abuse.

Seitz, S. (1989). Alienation: A false guide for solving sexual abuse cases. *Connections*, *3*, pp. 6-10.

Wisconsin psychologist Seitz wrote this short article after testifying in a case in which Gardner and his alienation hypothesis influenced the outcome, so that children were returned to live with a father whom they alleged to have sexually abused them. Seitz notes that Gardner's sexual abuse criteria findings have not been replicated in the literature and that his items do not constitute a "scale" that measures anything. She points out that many of Gardner's items do not take into account developmental differences among children (preschoolers, for example, may not show guilt about participating in sexual acts), differences in the nature of the abuse (children who have been traumatically abused or anally raped will not show sexual excitation), and the nature of child disclosures in confirmed cases (Gardner's 6th criterion states that in true cases, the child's description of the abuse does not vary, a criterion Seitz calls "absurd"). Seitz concludes, "Gardner's criteria, taken individually or collectively, neither prove nor disprove anything." She points out that ongoing abuse is often disclosed only at the time of marital separation. She adds that child advocacy has become more difficult since the "easy out" of claiming alienation has reached the courts, because "Most people, including some guardians and judges, would prefer to believe anything other than sexual abuse."

Seitz, S. (1990). Alienation: A toxic solution. *Connections*, *4*, pp. 6-7.

Seitz reiterates that Gardner's 26-item sexual abuse legitimacy checklist lacks the properties of a scale and has questionable psychometric value. She compares his checklist to others: those by Yates and Musty (1988) and Green (1986). She also criticizes Gardner's solution in cases of "alienation," which is to place the child with the parent from which it has been "alienated" and to allow no contact with the mother until the child has been "debriefed." She cites the attachment literature to warn of the dangers inherent in this disruption of a child's secure attachment to the primary parent and states that Gardner's recommendation is "irresponsible and cruel," especially for young children. She concludes that uncertainty in these difficult cases is preferable to premature and oversimplified guidelines and quotes Corwin that there are, indeed, "no easy answers."

Sheridan, R. (1990). The false child molestation outbreak of the 1980s: An explanation of the cases arising in the divorce context. *Issues in Child Abuse Accusations*, *2*(3), 146-151.

This article explores false allegations of child molestation in the context of divorce cases and discusses the use of a rational approach to understanding uncorroborated molestation charges developed by adults based on what children tell them following some not clearly understood behavior or appearance. The author cites the Salem witch-hunt of 1692 as the classic irrational child molestation case of all time.

He claims that children may similarly be pressured into an accusation of sexual abuse by a hostile mother during a divorce situation. Causes of false reports are examined, with the most common being the misinterpretation of a young child's account of an overnight visit with the father. Causes of the failure to detect false reports are considered, including the difficulty in obtaining the facts by ordinary investigative means. The author suggests that if emotionalism can be recognized and put aside, as the "rational" approach is focused on, valid cases can then be distinguished from invalid cases. He suggests that social workers and police investigators are unable to detect false reports and that "there is a tendency to lower the burden of proof to mere nothingness." He recommends that "in divorce cases, undue influence should be presumed until proven otherwise." It is unclear, however, what data the author uses as the basis of his conclusions, and no empirical support or evidence is apparent.

Sink, F. (1988). Studies of true and false allegation: A critical review. In E. B. Nicholson & J. Bulkley (Eds.), *Sexual abuse allegations in custody and visitation cases* (pp. 37-47). Washington, DC: American Bar Association.

Targeting professionals involved in dealing with sexual abuse allegations in the divorce context, this article reviews the dynamics, disclosure events, definitions, and findings regarding true and false allegations in cases of divorce involving child sexual abuse allegations.

The author points out that expanded research is needed in every aspect to make decisions in these "monumentally difficult" cases possible. Refined definitions of and theories regarding false allegations of sexual abuse as well as explanations for true disclosures in the divorce context and recommendations for assessment procedures are discussed. Notable information in this article includes summaries of theories involving false allegations, such as the overanxious parent, shared beliefs between parent and child, the suggestible child, and the response reinforcement theory. Other helpful information is the author's review of research studies regarding the frequency of false allegations.

Sirles, E. A., & Lofberg, C. (1990). Factors associated with divorce in intrafamily child sexual abuse cases. *Child Abuse & Neglect, 14,* 165-170.

This study analyzes factors related to the decision to divorce in intrafamilial sexual abuse cases. Data was collected on 128 cases of incest in St. Louis, Missouri, through the Washington University Child Guidance Center. Examination of multiple variables revealed differences between the families in intrafamilial child sexual abuse cases in which the parents elect to stay together versus those that divorce subsequent to the discovery of abuse. Families that broke up were more likely to have young child victims and have additional problems with domestic violence. The child was more likely to have revealed the abuse to the mother and to have been believed by her in divorcing cases.

Sivan, A. B. (1985). Preschool child development: Implications for investigation of child abuse allegations. *Child Abuse & Neglect, 15*, 485-493.

This article comprehensively reviews research and theories about normal child development as they pertain to the question of the veracity of reports made by children between the ages of 2 and 5. As the article states, "Examination of the research on children's thought and language, memory and learning, fears, fantasy, and play, as well as the research on the influence of television on children of this age, led to the conclusion that preschoolers base their play on the reality of their experience." She cites research that shows that heavy television viewing has an inverse relationship with imaginativeness. She states that research shows that exposure to television does not increase a child's creativeness of imagination.

Sivan concludes, "The rich fantasy life of the pre-schooler is overworked; it is a myth which perhaps was begun by Freud," and, "If this review accomplishes nothing else, we hope that the reader will remember that the constructions of preschoolers, whether in words or play, are not likely to be pure fantasy. More likely they are based on the reality of the child's experience, and the detail which they reflect is probably directly related to the amount of experience to which the child has been exposed."

Snyder, N. (1988). Who tells the truth about sexual abuse. *California Lawyer*, 8(3).

California attorney and author Neal Snyder addresses the widespread skeptical publicity flourishing about children being pressured into believing they were molested when they were not. He clearly states and describes research asserting the following points: "There is no wave of false allegations of child sexual abuse. Children cannot easily be manipulated to falsely believe they were molested. There is no scientific basis for treating the testimony of a child victim as inferior to other eyewitness testimony." Nevertheless, this publicity backlash has assisted in creating unjustified obstacles to the admission in recent California appellate cases of testimony by those who work with young victims of sexual abuse.

He suggests that the "California Court of Appeal was probably unaware of the research on children's testimony when it issued four decisions in 1987 that will hamper the introduction of expert testimony to support victim credibility in these cases. (In re: Sara M. 194 CA3d 585; Seering vs. Department of Social Services 194 CA3d 298; Amber B. 191 CA 3d 682; and Christine C. 191 CA3d 676)." In these cases, Snyder explains that "the appellate courts applied the Kelly-Fryee test to testimony about behavioral syndromes common to children who have been sexually abused, to opinions stemming from observation of a child's behavior with anatomically correct dolls and to the analysis of the child's statements. The Kelly-Fryee test says that testimony based on a scientific process is inadmissible without proof it is generally accepted as accurate in the relevant scientific community." Snyder goes on to show some leeway in applying this Kelly-Fryee test through the cases "People vs. Roscoe (1985) 1689 CA3d 1093; and People vs. Gray (1986) 187 CA3d 213."

The author objects to the use of this rule in child protective proceedings such as juvenile dependency cases, termination of parental rights cases, and proceedings to revoke licenses of facilities providing child care. The author states, "It is an insult to these judges for the appellate court to think they will attribute the aura of infallibility to testimony about characteristic victim behavior that a jury might attribute to a chemical test or computer analysis. The inappropriate application of the Kelly-Fryee usurps the Legislature's role in defining the admissibility of expert testimony, which is already adequately covered in the Evidence Code."

Sorenson, T., & Snow, B. (1991). How children tell: The process of disclosure in child sexual abuse. *Child Welfare*, *50*, 1-15.

This article studies disclosure patterns of over a hundred children in cases confirmed by perpetrator confession or physical evidence and serves as a caution to those such as the American Academy of Child and Adolescent Psychiatry who have published possible premature interview criteria to distinguish true from false allegations. Twenty-

two percent of Sorenson and Snow's sample retracted at
some point in the interview process, and over two thirds
did not disclose in the first interview. This is valuable
information on the process of children's disclosure.

Steward, M. S. (1992). Preliminary findings from the
    University of California/Davis Child Memory
    Study: Development and testing of interview pro-
    tocols for young children. *APSAC Advisor*, *5*(3),
    11-13.

   This is a presentation of preliminary findings from a
study of 3- to 6-year-old children's memories of a visit to
an outpatient clinic. The children were questioned immediately after the visit, 1 month later, and 6 months later. The
children reported only an average of 25% of what happened
to them, but the accuracy of their reports varied between
72% and 86%. When children reported the same information during all three interviews, the information was 25
times more likely to be accurate than inaccurate. The
authors also found that "children continued to report new
accurate information about body touch, including genital
touch, at one and six months." The authors express concern
about their finding that there was a subgroup of children
"who experienced painful invasive medical procedures but
later denied not only the distress, but even the body touch."
These children, however, had more accurate memory of the
persons present in the clinic room as compared to children
who underwent more benign procedures. This leads the
researchers to believe that the children did not forget the

painful experience. Further study of this phenomenon is hoped to lead to a better understanding of the underreporting by children who have been victims of abuse.

T

Thoennes, N. (1988). Child sexual abuse: Whom should a judge believe? What should a judge believe? *Judges Journal, 27*(3), 4-18, 48-49.

This article presents an overview of the findings of the 1988 study by the Denver-based research unit of the Association of Family and Conciliation Courts. The research included interviews of judges and court personnel in all 50 states, as well as in-depth studies in five court sites. Of the 9,000 custody-visitation disputes that were studied, slightly under 2% involved sexual abuse allegations. The results of evaluations by court investigators reveal that 50% of the allegations appear to be substantiated; in 17% of the cases, the validity could not be determined; in the remaining 33%, it was believed that the abuse had not happened. However, in most of the cases where it was concluded the abuse did not happen, the investigator felt that the allegation was made in good faith, based on genuine suspicions. The author concludes that "there is no evidence from the present research to suggest that a significant number of parents are using fabricated reports to win custody battles."

After studying the characteristics of individual cases in relationship to whether they were later substantiated, the author stresses that no single set of factors "allows for a simple determination." It is also pointed out that psychiatric evaluators may see a biased sample of cases because those with clear-cut evidence do not require a psychiatric evaluation. The article offers guidelines for psychiatric evaluators.

Thoennes, N. (1988). Jurisdictional issues between juvenile and domestic relations court. *Judges Journal*, *27*(3), 19, 53-54.

This article presents results from a 2-year study of sexual abuse allegations in custody cases, including surveys of members of the National Council of Juvenile and Family Court Judges and the Association of Family and Conciliation Courts. Most judges surveyed agreed that one court to handle both the custody dispute and the sexual abuse allegation would be preferred, but most acknowledged that the reorganization needed to create such a court is not likely. About 30% of court administrators and 25% of judges surveyed thought that division between juvenile and domestic relations courts sometimes hampered effective processing of cases. The exchange of information between the courts can expedite matters; in some jurisdictions the consolidation of cases is possible. Consolidating the cases before the juvenile bench is usually most successful. Some judges would like to see case consolidation including the criminal court as well. It is concluded that when consolidation is not possible, specialized sexual abuse teams in law enforcement or child protective services may help ensure smooth case processing. Delays can also be prevented by using court appointed special advocates (CASA) or guardians ad litem.

Thoennes, N., & Tjaden, P. G. (1990). The extent, nature, and validity of sexual abuse allegations in custody/visitation disputes. *Child Abuse & Neglect, 14,* 151-163.

This is the largest study completed to date on the rate of sexual abuse allegations in a sample of over 9,000 contested custody cases (less than 2%), false allegations (fewer than 20 in the entire sample), and so on. Information for the study was received by mail and telephone surveys, personal interviews with legal and mental health professionals, and empirical data from 12 domestic relations courts in the U.S. The study indicated that only a small proportion of contested custody and visitation cases involve sexual abuse allegations. In 169 cases for which data were gathered from court counselors, family court, and child protective service agency files, the data showed that accusations were brought by mothers, fathers, and third parties. In the 129 cases for which a determination of the validity of the allegation was available, 58% involved abuse, 33% involved no abuse, and 17% resulted in an indeterminate ruling. "48% of the cases involve a mother bringing accusations against the child's father and in another 6% of the cases the mother accuses her second husband of abusing her child by a former marriage. In the

latter cases the natural child whose custody is in dispute
has not been abused, but the alleged abuse of a stepchild
leads the mother to seek visitation restrictions."

The study found that in 10% of the cases, fathers
alleged that a child was sexually abused by the mother's
new male partner. In 6% of the cases, the mother herself
was accused of abuse. Nearly 20% of the cases involved
accusations by mothers (13%) or fathers (6%) against other
relatives and family friends. And in 11% of the cases, "the
allegation of sexual abuse clearly originated with someone
other than a parent, although in time parents may also
believe there was abuse. The third parties bringing these
allegations include relatives, especially grandmothers, or
mandated reporters, such as therapists, physicians or teach-
ers. The allegations brought by someone other than a parent
are equally likely to allege abuse by the child's father,
mother or her new partner, or another relative."

Four factors were significantly associated with the
perceived validity of the abuse report: victim's age, frequency of the alleged abuse, prior abuse/neglect reports,
and the time elapsing between filing for divorce and the
emergence of the allegation. The study resulted in the
consensus that sexual abuse allegations occur in a small
but growing number of cases.

It is a myth that sexual allegations are common in
custody disputes, with empirical data suggesting that from
1% to 8% of cases involve such allegations. Of these,
investigators estimated about half to be true. Data also
suggested that the stereotype that mothers falsely and
maliciously accuse fathers of abuse is unwarranted. Research further indicated that evaluation reports for the court

by mental health professionals can be valuable when well prepared. This investigation refuted the notions that allegations of sexual abuse are epidemic and that such allegations are most commonly made by a vindictive or impaired parent.

Toth, P. (1992). All child abuse allegations demand attention: A commentary. *Journal of Child Sexual Abuse, 1*, 117-118.

Attorney Toth agrees with Judge Schudson's commentary as having a "cogent and critical perspective too seldom aired" in this current climate of the child sexual abuse backlash. She points out that "the more disturbing tragedy is that most abuse is never reported," as indicated by considering the burgeoning adult survivor movement. Toth reminds us that child sexual abuse is a serious crime and that a report of child sexual abuse "no matter who is suspected or where it is raised, should be treated as an allegation of potentially serious criminal behavior and a potentially serious threat to a child's well-being and safety."

Toth recommends that, ideally, there should be an immediate referral to Child Protective Services and law enforcement to conduct a joint investigation that is prompt, thorough, and objective. "Skilled investigative interviews with all involved parties . . . should be combined with medical exams, searches for potential physical evidence, and all of the traditional criminal investigative techniques to supplement mental health or family court evaluations."

She emphasizes our need for more information, not less, to assist in discerning validity.

W

Wakefield, H., & Underwager, R. (1990). Personality characteristics of parents making false accusations of sexual abuse in custody disputes. *Issues in Child Abuse Accusations*, 2(3), 121-136.

A suggested typology of individuals who make false accusations of child sexual abuse in custody and divorce disputes is presented in this article. The authors suggest four overlapping categories of parents. The authors based this on the review of files in contested cases where there were false allegations. The personality characteristics of 72 falsely accusing parents and 103 falsely accused parents were compared with a control group of 67 parents involved in custody disputes without sexual abuse allegations. Wakefield and Underwager concluded that the accusing parents were much more likely than the two other groups to have a personality disorder such as borderline, histrionic, paranoid, or passive-aggressive. Only one quarter were seen as normal. In comparison, according to the authors most of the parents in the accused or custody-only groups were seen as normal.

Wakefield, H., & Underwager, R. (1991). Sexual abuse allegations in divorce and custody disputes. *Behavioral Sciences & The Law*, 9, 451-468.

The authors recognize the difficulties and complications of assessing child sexual abuse allegations during custody and divorce conflicts. They report that estimates of the rate of false allegations in custody disputes range from 20% to 80%. Sample biases in some of the studies reviewed, as well as inconsistencies in how an allegation is determined to be false, make these numbers difficult to interpret. The reader is cautioned "not to conclude immediately that an allegation is false simply because it arises in a divorce and custody dispute." The work of Faller, Corwin, Berliner, MacFarlane, Sink, and others delineating the reasons why genuine allegations of abuse may surface at the time of a divorce is reviewed. The authors recommend considering the following factors in differentiating between real and false allegations: the origin of the original disclosure, the timing of the allegation, the age of the child, the behavior of the accusing parent, the nature of the allegations, the characteristics of the child's statement, the personality characteristics of the parties involved, and the behavior of the professionals involved.

Wells, G. L., & Loftus, E. F. (1991). Commentary: Is this child fabricating? Reactions to a new assessment technique. In J. Doris (Ed.), *The suggestibility of children's recollections* (pp. 168-171). Washington, DC: American Psychological Association.

This chapter is a commentary on Raskin and Esplin's chapter on Criteria-Based Content Analysis (CBCA) that appears in the same volume. An annotation of Raskin and Esplin's chapter appears in this bibliography (see Raskin & Esplin, 1991). The authors of this commentary state that they "have concerns about CBCA with regard to the adequacy of its current empirical support, the ability of the technique to partition individual and age-related differences in linguistic abilities from validity-related differences, and the potential problem of overbelief of the results of CBCA on the part of judges and juries."

The Raskin and Esplin chapter discusses two studies on the reliability and validity of the CBCA. One of the studies compared the CBCA ratings of the disclosures made by alleged child victims of sexual abuse in "doubtful" and "confirmed" cases and found the CBCA scores to be significantly higher in the "confirmed cases." Wells and Loftus point out that the CBCA score is not corrected in any way for age-related linguistic abilities, and they question whether the differences found between the two groups might be due to age differences. In a reply to Wells and Loftus, the authors admitted that the children in the doubtful group were younger.

Another caution discussed was of the 20 "doubtful" cases involving statements that were invented by the children. Wells and Loftus state that the study included no independent corroboration for "invention" and no evidence that these children actually made up the abuse stories.

A related caution raised by Wells and Loftus is what they call "classification circularity," meaning that "the same factors that cause low scores on the CBCA [may] also cause the case to be classified as 'doubtful.' " The study described by Raskin and Esplin defined cases as doubtful on the basis of a lack of success in criminal prosecution and the absence of perpetrator confession. If these were cases involving younger, less developmentally mature children, they may not have been pursued in the legal system precisely because of the victims' limited ability to make a credible statement. Similarly, the perpetrators may have been less likely to confess because of their own awareness that the case might not go forward in the legal system. The authors comment that they "know of no good way to rule out this alternative interpretation."

Wells and Loftus conclude that the CBCA is in the preliminary stages of development and state that "we do not believe that the empirical data justify making conclusions of an absolute nature about individual cases." They go on to say that "after it receives more scientific support, and the kinds of problems that we have outlined have been addressed, CBCA might be justified as a powerful technique for courtroom use." (For another commentary on the Raskin and Esplin chapter, see McGough, 1991).

White, S., Santilli, G., & Quinn, K. (1988). Child evaluators' roles in child sexual abuse assessments. In E. B. Nicholson, & J. Bulkley (Eds.), *Sexual abuse allegations in custody and visitation cases* (pp. 94-105). Washington, DC: American Bar Association.

White, Santilli, and Quinn explain that "in the assessment of child sexual abuse cases, the roles of the child evaluator, regardless of discipline, must be considered within the context of legal issues." The authors state that "the child evaluator must approach the assessment of sexual abuse cases in such a way as to collect data for the judicial system which will be as free of professional contamination as possible." The authors go on to say that "the evaluator is to view themselves [sic] as an investigatory interviewer not the trier of fact or therapist." This paper attempts to clarify some specific attitudes and roles that should be considered, such as independence, neutrality, and an established set of procedures followed in each case. Contrary to current APSAC and Academy guidelines, the authors recommend a blind evaluation. Further issues addressed include the referral, contacts during the evaluation, time constraints, financial considerations, parent management, child management, environment of the interview, free play period, developmental skills, and the abuse evaluation with consideration for rule-outs.

Williams, L. M. (1992). Adult memories of childhood abuse: Preliminary findings from a longitudinal study. *APSAC Advisor, 5*(3), pp. 19-21.

The author conducted a follow-up study of 100 women who had been examined at a community hospital subsequent to a report of sexual abuse when they were young children in the early 1970s. The women were told that this was a study of those who had received health services at the hospital. During the course of the interview, they were queried as to whether they had ever been sexually abused. The women were also asked whether they were aware of any sexual abuse reports that may have been made about them in which the abuse did not actually occur.

The study found that 38% of the women did not remember their sexual victimization or chose not to report it to the interviewer. Approximately half of the women who did not describe the particular event of abuse that brought them into the study did remember another incident of abuse during their childhood. The implications of these findings for conclusions about the prevalence of child sexual abuse and the long-term effects of abuse are discussed.

Williams, L. M., & Finkelhor, D. (1988). The characteristics of incestuous fathers: A review of recent studies. In W. L. Marshall, D. R. Laws, & H. E. Barbaree, *The handbook of sexual assault: Issues, theories and treatment of the offender*. New York: Plenum.

This still useful literature review gives statistics on child physical and sexual abuse histories, concurrent battering, and test data on fathers who sexually abuse. It provides some correlations of physical abuse by fathers, battering by father to mother, and poor relationships with one's father as present in offenders.

Wolfe, V. V., Gentile, C., & Wolfe, D. A. (1989). The impact of sexual abuse on children: A PTSD formulation. *Behavior Therapy, 20,* 215-228.

The authors of this study suggest that posttraumatic stress disorder provides a useful framework for conceptualizing the variety of symptoms that are often seen as a result of sexual victimization. They administered a number of measures to 71 children between the ages of 5 and 16 years who were assessed by a child protection agency. The sample consists of only confirmed cases of abuse. These children scored more than one standard deviation above the normative sample on the PTSD scale of the Child Behavior Checklist. Another measure, the Children's Impact of Traumatic Events Scale—Revised (CITES), revealed that these children suffer from repeated intrusive, ruminating thoughts about the abuse and that they are more likely to harbor a general belief that adults exploit children. The results are interpreted to support the contention that the PTSD construct is a useful tool for understanding the effects of sexual abuse on children.

Yuille, J. C. (1988). The systematic assessment of children's testimony. *Canadian Psychology*, *29*, 247-261.

Yuille reviews the experimental and case study litera-ture about child witnesses and concludes that carefully interviewed children are as capable of providing accurate accounts of events as are adults. Although he concludes that research shows that the evidence is clear that children are competent to provide testimony, he states, as Goodman and others have also found, that the younger the child, the less information the child will be able to recall. On the separate issue of credibility, and what Yuille describes as the "disproportionate weight" now given to children's statements, he offers a model for distinguishing the major-ity of valid disclosures from the minority (he estimates them at less than 10%) of invalid ones. (Yuille does not clearly distinguish between unfounded, mistaken, and fab-ricated abuse disclosures, which leads to some confusion in his argument.) He offers Undeutsch's Statement Reality Analysis (renamed Statement Validity Analysis—SVA) as developed by Stellar and Koehnken of the University of Kiel, Raskin at the University of Utah, and Yuille himself of the University of British of Columbia.

Yuille then describes SVA, which includes a nondi-rective, videotaped clinical interview. He recommends against the use of anatomically detailed dolls. He then offers the evaluative "heart" of SVA, which is the Statement Analysis Protocol and the Validity Checklist. He describes the application of SVA to children's testimony as "promising." He does not, however, address how the interview technique and statement analysis should be adjusted for children at different developmental stages.

About the Authors

WENDY DEATON is a licensed Marriage, Family, and Child Counselor with a private practice in San Luis Obispo, California. Wendy holds a B.A. from the University of California, Santa Barbara, and an M.A. from the University of Redlands, Johnston College. She has also pursued graduate studies at Oregon State University and California Graduate Institute, Los Angeles. Wendy has served as a mediator for Family Court Services in cases of custody and visitation and is the author of two professional articles in the field of victimology and coauthor of a therapeutic book series for children.

SUZANNE LONG is a Board Certified Diplomate in clinical social work in private practice in Newport Beach, California. She is the coauthor of *Sexual Abuse of Young Children: Evaluation and Treatment* and a recognized trainer and consultant in the area of child and adolescent psychotherapy. She has been working in the field for over 25 years and divides her work between children and adults with a variety of problems, particularly specializing in play therapy and parent/child issues. She is on the board of directors of CAPSAC.

HOLLY MAGAÑA is a licensed psychological assistant in private practice at the Center for the Family in Santa Ana, California, and has prior experience as a child custody mediator for the Superior Court of the County of Orange, California. She holds B.A. and doctorate degrees from the University of California, Irvine and has pursued additional graduate studies in clinical psychology at Pepperdine University and United States International University. Dr. Magaña teaches a course on child abuse at the University of California in Irvine. She has trained and published in the area of family violence and child custody mediation.

JULIE ROBBINS is a Licensed Clinical Social Worker and has been doing psychotherapy, training, consultation, and program development in the field of child abuse and family violence for the past 15 years. Julie holds a B.A. degree from Oberlin College and received her M.S.W. from the University of Chicago. Ms. Robbins has a private practice in San Francisco, where she works with adults and children, consults at a homeless youth program, and teaches a child development and child abuse course at a local Bay Area university. She is on the Board of Directors of CAPSAC, where she has served as the chairperson for the Task Force on Sexual Abuse Allegations in Custody Disputes.